I0029292

# A Short History

## of

# Political Thinking

*By the Same Author:*

Intelligence in Politics

Sovereignty

The Fields and Methods
of Knowledge
*with R. F. Piper*

# A Short History

## of

# Political Thinking

PAUL W. WARD, PH.D.

*Professor of Philosophy
in Syracuse University*

Chapel Hill

THE UNIVERSITY OF NORTH CAROLINA PRESS

1939

Copyright, 1939, by

The University of North Carolina Press

The University of North Carolina Press, Chapel Hill, N. C.;
The Baker & Taylor Company, New York; Oxford University
Press, London; Maruzen-Kabushiki-Kaisha, Tokyo; Edward
Evans & Sons, Ltd., Shanghai; D. B. Centen's Wetenschappelijke
Boekhandel, Amsterdam.

To

My Mother and Father

## FOREWORD

There seems to be a place for a small outline history of political thinking both to serve the interests of the general reader and to accompany lectures and assigned readings in original sources for beginning students. Advanced students also frequently find a compact summary useful for purposes of review. These considerations have motivated the writing of this manual.

Throughout the chapters I have borrowed materials freely and have emphasized by their selection the points of view which I regard as most significant. My colleagues, Professors H. W. Peck, H. C. Beyle, R. V. Harlow, W. F. Galpin, C. G. Haines, and W. B. Walsh have read parts of the typescript; they, of course, do not share responsibility for any errors. My wife has helped at various points, with critical and mechanical assistance.

P. W. W.

# CONTENTS

"Let no state believe that it can always follow a safe policy, rather let it think that all are doubtful."

—Machiavelli, *The Prince*.

## CHAPTER I

# INTRODUCTION

There are tides in the affairs of men, ebbs and flows of human events, which have been recurrent since human life began. Much of the time things have just happened; but sometimes, and more especially in the recent past, they have both happened and been thought about. When social events not only occur but also are reflected upon, there arises political thinking. In the broadest sense this involves all significant utterances in reference to all bodies of social action since the invention of language. Men have been thinking about their collective affairs continuously since they became articulate. Of most of this there are no records, even from the days since writing first became a popular accomplishment. Such records as do exist, therefore, assume a greater significance when recognized as representatives, now good, now bad, of the many inarticulate gropings and unwritten utterances of large numbers of men in their respective ages.

A history of political thinking might be interminable. If an attempt were made to compass all known political and social utterances, an encyclopedic work would be the result. Many repetitions and much triviality would be discovered, even if attention were confined to the most important periods of social development. The beginner must take up his study at some particular point, and he most profitably begins by studying the most representative thinkers. Every age has had its problems ; that thinker has been great who has stated those problems precisely and attempted their solution deliberately. Such a thinker has become representative of his age. To understand the doctrines of the great immortals makes possible a deeper insight into the many muddled pools of logic in the subsequent bayous of history. "The works of those who have stood the tests of ages have a claim to that respect and veneration to which no modern can pretend."

Perhaps there is the antecedent question of why one should undertake the study of political thinking at all. Disraeli is reported to have said in true romantic fashion that all the noblest of human actions spring from the passions. If one accepts this, why should one bother about what men have said concerning their problems? Why study their reasoning if their noblest statements of purpose were the expression of their hidden inarticulate motives? Why, indeed, should one study political thinking?

Even without begging the question as to the rôle of reason, it may be said that passions have their histories. To study the careers of passions is to gain illumination, apart from any logical systems in terms of which they may be stated. And, if what men say is in any sense evidence of their perennial needs, political utterances have deep significance. The beginner, of course, may approach political thinking, or any other form of thinking, with merely an antiquarian curiosity. It may be studied just for the fun of it; this type of interest, when refined and equipped, is the pure-research interest in political philosophy. The pure science of historical interpretation is akin to fine art. But there are more practical motives which may be operative. Whatever we may find political thinking to have been, the solutions which men have given to their social problems in the past may be of help to men in contemporary society. The formulas of bygone days may enlarge the imagination of the present and make men enlightened in confronting contemporary crises in society. All action may originate in impulse, but it becomes noble only by being intelligent.

If, however, we study social and political philosophy in the hope of reaching a final solution for all social problems, some formula which will always cure every social ailment, then we are doomed to disappointment. The political and social theories of men always concern the problems of their culture and age, and are to be understood only in that context. Such theories are attempted solutions of those problems, taken in the widest sense, and, when properly understood, may help all succeeding ages to enlightened social action. When they are misunderstood, social thinking can be worse than useless, for, like the drugs used by the medical profession, social formulas have their specific uses. Everything excellent is both difficult and rare; the proper understanding and employment of our social experience is no exception.

There are many difficulties involved in achieving

even a rudimentary knowledge of the field. Most of these
difficulties cluster around the chief aim of the enterprise; that is, to see what each man means to say about
his society. He must be allowed to say what he wants
to say, not what someone else may think he should have
said about some society in which he might have lived
but did not. Therefore, to be punctilious in matters of
interpretation requires a very considerable knowledge
of records other than those of the critical comments
concerning the social forms which are to be interpreted.
The historian of political thought should have knowledge as encyclopedic as possible of all records pertain-
ing to the various cultures within which the thinkers
whom he is studying were living. There is, at this point,
a limit to the possibility of human achievement, both
because of the paucity of human records and of the
inability of one man to grasp so much material. Each
great thinker is, in fact, a whole field of human knowledge. The student of political thinking must lean upon
the previous work of men who are deeply specialized in
the historical study of the records of various ages.

Every cultural pattern is a complex of trends. Certain
frameworks of rights and duties, virtues and vices, rules
and laws, have existed which must be understood as
frames of reference. What movements are taking place
within these frames of reference? What groups within
the various societies are changing in status? What im-
pacts are coming from without? The practical movements of the various ages must be envisaged, for it

is with these that the thinking of the political writer is concerned.

Ideas, in other words, are about a society. The historian of ideas who would make his story of human wants, needs, and interests complete should know the society as well as the ideas. Sometimes the ideas are merely rationalizations of the existing order in a society, merely *ex post facto* descriptions, eulogistic or justificatory in character. Or, they may be partly this and partly suggestions of changes to be made. Again, the writer may describe his own society to condemn it, perhaps turning away from it to sketch an ideal society in which great wrongs are to be righted. He may be justifying a revolution still to come, rather than one which has been. But even the dreams of the wildest dreamer reflect the contemporary scene. One cannot know what the writer means unless one knows the cultural set-up within which the utterances are made. Only as a result of such knowledge can the ideas used become meaningful, and their exponent stand out as a dramatic living reality. The blood and dust of conflict must be sensed or the diction of the writer will be merely quaint and flat. The understanding of a political thinker is just begun when we find out what he said; it may never be completed.

While motives may be obscure, and results frequently unintended, in political thinking great human needs and wants are always at stake. To clarify and adjust conflicting human interests is the business of the political thinker and the statesman in every age. Today can profit by knowing the successes and failures of yesterday. Without such historical depth scientific method is impotent and social advancement can be only an accident.

## CHAPTER II

## GREEK CITY-STATE

Societies existed before they were criticized. Prior to the emergence of any sort of knowledge, primitive social groupings existed. Behind the very earliest of recorded utterances lay the social order of neolithic men. In the subsequent poetry of the Bronze Age we can see men beginning to become aware of what they were doing. They discovered the various existing forms of social action just as they discovered their diseases. While it is perhaps true that we are still in the process of discovery, we have, nevertheless, in contrast to primitive societies, a large amount of recently invented differentiation among our social activities. Primitive social activities were simple, homogeneous, undifferentiated. Activities we call family, school, business, church, club, profession, and government either did not exist or were tied together closely; the same person or persons might be head of all of them at the same time.

Most early writings give evidence of the continuing simplicity of primitive structure. Oriental cultures even today have not freed themselves from the earlier undifferentiated attitudes of primitive men. Theological and political factors, for example, remain confused. The Jews, Saracens, and Chinese got a little further temporarily, but at no time did they achieve that high degree of differentiation characteristic of the most ad-

2

vanced cultures of the contemporary Occident. Europe itself, of course, cannot claim an unbroken career. After the brilliant social developments of the classical and Hellenistic periods, that continent relapsed for a time into neolithic stupidity on social affairs as upon most others. Social and political thinking, and culture in general, had to be reborn.

Political theory, in the strict meaning of the term, began when men became reflectively aware of their governmental structures as such. To the ancient Greeks belongs the credit for the invention of social thinking in this sense. Egyptian, Babylonian, Cretan, Jewish—all previous cultures—had failed to make the distinction which the Greeks achieved. Although the incoming Hellenes had assimilated Minoan culture in some degree, they seem never to have become orientalized in their thinking. The posterity of the Homeric heroes had the mark of primitive groupings upon them; family, clan, tribe were important in the aristocracies of the early classical period. They were so important that devices were employed by democratic leaders to neutralize their influence, as when Cleisthenes organized the demes. But the theocratic, lethargic, oriental despotisms were entirely foreign to them. They developed a city life. With the appearance of commerce and sea power, the Greek middle ages came to an end and the brilliant classical period began. The tyrant appeared, by whom no religious, conventional, or institutional support was claimed. Arbitrary secular government had been invented. The

tyrant ruled unblushingly, so long as he could retain
the power.

The development of Greece was peculiar. Small communities were self-governing and changed their governors and governments frequently. The transitory tyrant
found it difficult to claim direct descent from divinities;
religious justification for seizing the power became a
little too obviously propaganda. Furthermore, no extensive ecclesiastical organization was developed to become self-conscious, ambitious, and jealous of its power.
So politics, and in some sense everything else, came to be
discussed in its own right for the first time. The smallness
of the Greek city-state, its rapidly changing social
scenery, the intensity of the conflicts within it—all these
facilitated the development of self-consciousness. Town
life had grown rapidly in the seventh and six centuries,
and each little city had developed its own life, with peculi-
arities of dress, manners, and craftsmanship. There were
internal feuds, either based on old family groupings or
rising economic class distinctions, and external wars of
varying intensities. The Greek was forced to think, and
think hard, about society. He was not irreligious; political events simply moved so rapidly that religious ones
were presumed to be forgotten. The grandiose formulas
of theology seemed thin and far off when the question
concerned who was to be tyrant tomorrow. Classical
Greece was, indeed, a veritable political laboratory;
microscopic societies were changing with kaleidoscopic
rapidity. The Greek was so bedeviled by his social prob-

lems that he forgot to worry about his theological ones. When reflectively discussed, religion was thought of as a means of strengthening the city-state rather than as an end in itself. At all events, from the time of the tyrant in ancient Greece, secular theories of government were present. Following the Persian wars came an increased wave of popular government, resisted by the aristocratic groups under the leadership of Sparta. The Golden Age of Greece was here. Even international ideas arose; among the city-states leagues developed with varying commitments and changing hegemonies.

The background of the Greek city-state was, of course, predominantly agrarian. The citizens had what we should call today an agrarian and consumer ideology. They possessed the sturdy democratic susceptibilities of retired farmers. In spite of the fact that Athens at her height had from 300,000 to 400,000 population, only half lived in the urban area, and of these only about 40,000 were citizens. Trade and industry, still on a very small scale and largely in the hands of metics, were regarded by the citizens merely as a source of taxation and of the provisions necessary to maintain the body of citizens. The Greek cities of the Golden Age were not the instruments of economic motives in any capitalistic sense. They were not seeking outlets for manufactured articles. The city was regarded rather as an instrument of the citizen's ideal of a life without labor. Slaves did the manual labor; metics managed the business. The citizen should be free to live the good life. The military activities, public service, art, the enjoyments of life—these should employ the leisure of the citizen. Greek democracy developed from a peasantry. Greek imperialism, when it developed, was aimed toward tribute and the control of supplies to support the citizenry. Life was still ancient; economy was municipal, almost domestic, always agrarian.

Accompanying the appearance of tyranny in Greece there arose the Sophists. These men were prominent in the city life of the fifth century. They formulated a tradition which in substance provided a justification for the ruthlessness of the tyrant. The Sophists were the first who took money for teaching and pretended to be able to tell young men how to get along in the world. Theirs was a philosophy of complete disillusionment. Many of them had traveled widely, and the relativity of customs and social standards had impressed them. They announced both the secularity and the conventionality not only of political affairs but of all morality as well. They went to the extreme length of championing anarchic individualism—law was the power of the strongest. The wise citizen, therefore, should prepare himself for action and defense in court, and in his life as a whole, so that he should play the superman rather than be played upon by others.

This radical development, a kind of ancient Nietzscheanism which must have sounded pleasant to the ears of tyrants, aroused the citizens. It also antagonized aristocratic thinkers who were on the right wing, so to speak, of current political opinion. Socrates (469-399 B.C.), as pictured by Plato, criticized most stringently the doctrines of the Sophists; yet he seems to have been forced to drink the hemlock by the Athenian democracy in the rôle of an arch-Sophist. If he is to be classed as a Sophist he is easily the noblest Sophist of them all. He saw through the tangled thinking of the Sophists and perceived that there were many things that mattered a great deal in society and that by definition and careful thinking much might be accomplished. Nevertheless, he wrote nothing; and it was as a corruptor of youth and an apostate to religion that he met his death. Incensed public opinion simply got the wrong man; the citizens were really defending their state. They resented criticism from both left and right, and Socrates in his memorable defense was either too preoccupied or too proud to make his best case before the jury. He really believed the state was not conventional but natural and inevitable, that law was sacred (he refused to escape, after his conviction, out of deference to the laws of Athens), that right is superior to force, that society is prior to the individual, and that those in public service should be the wisest and best of men.

All these were useful doctrines in the Greek scene at the end of the fifth century. What Greece needed was peace, integration, and wisdom at the helm of affairs, rather than a host of ambitious young citizens pruning themselves for the career of tyrant. In the latter direction lay anarchy and social dissolution; and, sad to relate, that was the way Greece went.

Yet Socrates did not die in vain. His great pupil Plato (427-347 B.C.), as well as Xenophon, described his life and doctrines. So thoroughly did he leave his mark on the former that it has since been a perennial puzzle how much of the famous Platonic canon represents the ideas of Socrates and how much is due exclusively to his pupil. Plato was an aristocrat in family, with the royal blood of the last of the old kings of Athens in his veins, as well as that of Solon the great lawgiver. As a youth he came under the influence of Socrates and studied with him for the eight years prior to the latter's death. At that event he fled the city of Athens and traveled to Megara, Cyrene, Egypt, and southern Italy for more than a decade. He returned to found the Academy and to spend the rest of his life in teaching and writing, interrupted by his adventure at Syracuse.

Subject to the exigencies of the influence of Megarian and Pythagorean doctrine, Plato's teachings took the direction of expounding and applying the seminal suggestions of Socrates: that intellect should be primary in man, that knowledge and morality were in a broad sense identical, and that the supreme goal of man should be virtue. He attacked both the anarchism of sophistic reasoning and the equalitarian assumptions of the Athenian democracy. Indeed, all existing forms of government were condemned by him as he developed the doctrine that only knowledge can help and pleaded magnificently for government by the expertly educated. Plato was an aristocrat to the end, but at the end it was an aristocracy not of wealth, birth, or force, but of knowledge and virtue which claimed his allegiance.

His vision of government by the educated has had a peculiar charm for subsequent ages, although it never has been tried systematically.

Plato's chief political dialogue, and perhaps his greatest, is the *Republic*. His *Statesman* and *Laws* are also important; the latter is gaining increasing recognition as a source and background for Roman juristic evolution. The *Republic* poses the central political question of justice. Why so much injustice in the world? What is justice? The position of the Sophists is stated by one Thrasymachus who is made to appear silly by the strictures of Socrates. The latter then proceeds to develop the argument that the good life is one lived in society, that justice can exist only within the organic unity of a city and then only by virtue of the organization of that city into a harmonious balance of functions.

How can this harmonious organization of functions be achieved? In answering this question, Plato illustrates the importance of psychology for all ethical and social thinking, for he turns to a theory of human motives as the basis for his constructive teaching. Men naturally have various motives, he says, some higher (above the diaphragm) and some lower. Those men who are dominated by lower sensual impulses naturally constitute the working class of a city. Appetites characterize them, and temperance is their best virtue. Above this class should be those dominated by higher motives, the spirited warriors, characterized by courage and the aggressive out-moving motives. From these, by a process of educational selection, a merit system of election, the magistrates should be chosen. The warriors as a group should be trained until twenty years of age, and those selected to be rulers should be given further education until thirty-five; then fifteen years of duty in governmental posts will fit them, at the age of fifty, for magistracy. The "perfect guardians," or rulers, are these intellectuals, who form a third class over and above the warriors; the latter are designated as "guardians" or "auxiliaries." A three-class society results, which is based upon a logical classification of human motives, and is thought of as subjected to an intense educational discipline. Justice is the harmonious operation of the life of these three classes in the city.

Not only is the educational system of the *Republic* significant (Plato's Academy was the first European university), but Plato's treatment of the economic and family relations of his guardian and ruling classes is strikingly at variance with the practice of the Greek society of his day. His utopianism is most vivid at this point; for, in his effort to enhance the attachment which these citizens are to have for their city, he demolishes their family life and eliminates the privacy of their property. All possessions and children are had in common by the men and women of the guardian and ruler class.

From this communism Plato retreats in his *Statesman* and *Laws*. His thought becomes more adjusted to the traditions of his day and the possibilities of their development. The *Statesman* suggests that a philosopher-king might be the best solution, while in the *Laws* Plato retreats still farther from his ideal state and indicates that a mixed constitution with separate and divided powers is the best attainable polity.

Plato, the first of the great immortals of man's intellectual life, was followed immediately by another in the person of his pupil Aristotle (384-322 B.C.). The latter was not an Athenian by birth, but was a native of Stagira, a city of Thrace, and the son of a physician at the court of Philip of Macedonia. As a youth Aristotle attached himself to the Academy and studied under Plato until the latter's death in 347 B.C. Thereupon he left and, for a short time, was attached to the court of a princeling in Asia Minor, whence he went to Macedonia and became the tutor of the young Alexander, son of Philip. For three years he ran a school at the court of Philip. When Alexander succeeded to the throne, Aristotle returned to Athens, founded the Lyceum (the second European university), and taught for more than a decade during the vicissitudes of his pupil's meteoric career. The death of Alexander exposed Aristotle to the attacks of the anti-Macedonian party in Athens, and he fled the city that it might not repeat the crime against philosophy which it had committed in executing Socrates. He retired to Chalcis, where he died.

Aristotle's works have not come down to us in published form, as have the Platonic dialogues. They are not finished literary productions but seem to be notes, either from which he lectured or from the notebooks of his auditors. His *Politics*, for example, contains three sets of lectures which careful critics have uncovered by internal criticism; one commentator maintains that five treatises went into its making. The major content of his doctrine seems to have been preserved, although ancient lists of his published works indicate titles of which we are unfortunately ignorant. We know he made a collection of one hundred and fifty-eight written constitutions of various states, only one of which, that of Athens, survives. The whole of the Aristotelian canon lacks the literary charm of Plato's polished phrases.

The excellence of the man's thought, however, is revealed by the fact that, in spite of the haphazard character of much of his surviving material, subsequent generations have recognized in it a first-rate body of doctrine. Aristotle was *the* philosopher for generations in the Middle Ages, even when some of his best literary remains were either unknown or misunderstood. For our purposes, the *Nicomachean Ethics* and the *Politics* are the chief documents, for in them Aristotle is confronting, as did his teacher, the joint problem of the moral life and the nature of social organization.

Aristotle was a more democratic thinker than Plato. There was less of the aristocrat and dreamer and more of the equalitarian and practical politician in his attitude. An approvable morality he defines as the moderate exercise of man's natural aptitudes, issuing in happiness. Virtue lies in the mean between excesses. The brave man is neither cowardly nor foolhardy; the liberal man is neither prodigal nor penurious. This famous ethical doctrine of the "golden mean" Aristotle applied to politics. The city should observe it also, if it expected to be durable; his equally famous doctrine of the middle class resulted. The wise legislator should conserve his middle class, eliminating the very wealthy, who become irresponsible, as well as the very poor, who become brutalized by their poverty. The middle class should be larger than either of the other classes, preferably larger than both other classes put together.

Aristotle repudiates Plato's communism in strongest terms. How much better really to be even a cousin of someone than a father or son after the manner of Plato! Aristotle finds in the family the basis of society, a natural group organized to care for man's daily needs. From it, through the village, develops the city, a natural growth originating in the needs of life but continuing for the purpose of "the good life." In Athens he saw the most brilliant example of the self-sufficing autonomous community.

All of Aristotle's thinking is cast in terms of the city-state. He indicates that its size should be no larger than the number of men who can be taken in at a single view. He speaks of its large slave community, its public worship, its laws. He classifies all existing governmental forms and finally champions the constitutional republic as the best of all possible forms for the city. If an all-wise king could be secured, monarchy would be desirable; but where can such a one be found? Any form of government must be protected by an educational system adapted to the constitution, of course. The young must be brought up to observe the rules laid

down in the constitution or it cannot endure. After
making a masterly analysis of the causes of revolutions,
Aristotle concludes that a large middle class and a
proper system of education are the best preventives of
such dire social convulsions.

Either he did not see what his illustrious pupil,
Alexander, was accomplishing, or he felt that it was
temporary, or perhaps as undesirable as were the
oriental despotisms. What may he not have thought
about political affairs in the years following the rise
of Alexander's empire? Aristotle's Macedonian connec-
tions embroiled him with his fellow Athenians. But on
the face of the record, as with Socrates, this un-
popularity was undeserved. He was the best friend and
the most constructive critic the Greek city-state of his
day possessed.

## CHAPTER III

# ROMAN EMPIRE

Both Plato and Aristotle, greatly as they differed on points of theory concerning the Greek city-state, agreed that proper civic education could save it. They were mistaken. There was too much internal corruption, too much brutal oppression of smaller states by their more powerful neighbors, too many costly and protracted wars. War ever has been the Nemesis of human cultures. Party strife and the slowness of inter-city organization sealed the fate of the nation. The federalism which might have saved it came too late.

Only a civic education involving a total reconstruction of Greek life could have saved the day. The city-state as it existed could not survive; but, like many a later social order, it reached its best intellectual formulation when it had already fallen into decay. The Macedonian invasion annexed Greece to Macedonia in 338 B.C. and the career of Alexander began two years later. It ended in Babylon in 323 B.C. Events moved swiftly. The social order of the whole eastern Mediterranean basin was thrown into the melting-pot of war so rapidly that even the most careful criticisms of its previous structures were pathetically out-of-date within a decade. Alexander spread Greek language and culture, at least a thin veneer of it, east as far as the

Indus, engulfing all existing polities from there to the
Adriatic in one great military empire.

The results were revolutionary for the Greek. Instead of deliberating about his destiny, speculating
about the good life, on the assumption that somehow
it was within his grasp if he could but solve his immediate problems, he began to feel the bewilderment
of a man confronting an earthquake. Little as had been
the impact of the great thinkers upon the practical
affairs of the city-states, life had nevertheless been regarded as a chess game to be played and possibly won.
Now the board had been removed and the pieces, even
the pawns, were beyond the grasp of the Greek citizen.
At first the schools of Athens refused to believe it. They
went on talking about the city-state, repeating the teachings of their great founders as though there had been no
intervening cataclysm. They reminiscently citicized that
state on which had been centered all their hopes and
fears, sorrows and pleasures. It had been their life, their
faith, their hope; and they would not believe that it was
to be no more.

The advent of Rome did not change the confused
situation. The individual had been cut loose from his
local moorings. What could give his life a purpose?
What could be his goal in such a vast imperial order?
Alexander's empire broke up at his death into three
pieces, under the control of three of his generals; but
Macedonia and Greece came under Roman control in
149 B.C., the empire of the descendants of Seleucus in

64 B.C. and that of the Ptolemies in 30 B.C. The glory
that was Greece was gone. Rome was the residuary
legatee of the military imperialism so brilliantly sym-
bolized in the figure of Alexander. What could a Greek
who tried to be reflectively civilized think about such a
world? Political and social thinking declined steadily
for generations immediately following 322 B.C. How
would the Greek mind resolve the problem?

Beside the decadent tradition of the Athenian schools
still postulating the city-state as the last word in social
theory, there emerged two new answers. Both of these
admitted that the city-state was gone, never to return,
and attempted a restatement of what life meant and
what men should do in that great imperial basin of
Hellenistic culture. The founders of these philosophies
were not Athenian. Epicurus (340-270 B.C.) was born
on Samos, went to Athens to study, and joined the
Academy. Zeno (340-260 B.C.) came from Cyprus, and
his father was a Phoenician. Although he also studied
at Athens, there is little of the city-state in his doctrine.

Epicurus picked up that third major tradition of
Greek thought, rivaling Platonism and Aristotelianism,
the atomism of the great Democritus. Using this, with
Cyrenaic and Sophistic modifications, he achieved a
new synthesis. If the Greeks at their best had been
without a priesthood, and had taken their theology *cum
grano salis,* it must be said of Epicurus that he became
definitely anticlerical in his position. The classic Greeks
had not bothered to be anticlerical; for them their

religion had been a beautiful and poetic medium within which they had moved about freely by way of critical speculation. But with the decline of the city-state, the cult life and organized priesthoods assumed a new significance in local communities. If the rising young men could not become politicians and tyrants, they could at least become priests. At all events, Epicurus goes out of his way to attack religions as pure fictions, under the influence of which all sorts of enormities had been committed. Only the particular individual mattered, said Epicurus, and pleasure was his goal; he should get as much of it out of life as possible. The state was but a means to this good life of the individual; it was an artificial creation, a convention, based on contract. Law has no obligation other than utility; the type of government matters but little, so long as peace is preserved and the individual is afforded elbow room in which to move about and live his life without undue commotion.

This type of teaching lent itself to various interpretations. Epicurus kept it on a high plane; the pleasures of science and art were stressed by him. Even at best it was social acquiescence to the inevitable. What other attitude could a Greek assume in a Roman world? But, at its worst, Epicureanism became antisocial and an apology for personal irresponsibility and viciousness in conduct. The appeal to pleasure could cover a multitude of misdemeanors. In general, the doctrine did not exert a strong appeal to the Roman ruling class. Why should it have done so? They did not have to acquiesce. Its only Latin expressions are the *De Rerum Natura* of Lucretius and the poetry of Horace.

Stoicism, the answer alternative to Epicureanism, was one which appealed to the Romans, to the ruling class as well as to the more humbly placed. Marcus Aurelius, Seneca, Epictetus—the followers of the Stoa ranged from emperor to slave. The teachings of this school influenced Christianity. By the time the latter assumed political importance within the Roman Empire, considerable portions of Stoic doctrine had been absorbed by it, directly or indirectly. Stoic tradition harked back to the Cynics, to Socrates and Heraclitus. Pleasure was not the goal, but duty. Desires should be held in check, and the expression of emotion should be avoided; indeed, the key to happiness for the individual lay in the reduction of his desires rather than in their gratification. It mattered not at all what one's position in society might be; wherever one was, his desires should be less than he could fulfill. By such reserve, or apathy, life could best be met. Stoicism did not argue that one should feel emotion and pass that emotion over into intelligent action; it said rather that one should not feel at all. Hence it moved in the direction of austerity, coldness, even asceticism. It offered, as contrasted to the cultivated Epicurean pleasures, the alternative of a cold and compelling duty. A certain element of acquiescence was present, as in Epicureanism, but also there was a certain imperative. The ambiguities of the system came to a focus in Stoicism's idea of nature. They never were completely resolved. Indeed, the very ambiguity of its concepts may account, in part, for the fact that some diluted form of Stoicism has been the most popular philosophy in the western world up to the present day.

Nature was thought of as a rational order; the law of nature was eternal and supreme. Its mandates took precedence over all positive legal enactments. It was a providential, rational order, objective, eternal, universal; to be just was to be in harmony with it. In other words, nature involved both what was and what ought to be. To acquiesce was to accept the naturally inevitable; to achieve what ought to be also was in accordance with the law of nature. The scope of such a doctrine was very wide. If active and in control, one had the law of nature on one's side to justify what seemed expedient. If at the limit of one's powers, acquiescence was imperative, but it was acquiescence to the supreme rational order of nature. Almost anything can be done with these terms by way of justifying attitudes and conduct; and, historically, almost everything has been done.

The phase of Stoicism which appealed to the Roman ruling class seems to have been this universal aspect of it. Not merely the ethical aspects of it interested the Roman; its political uses were even more important. He was confronted with the problem of organizing a host of diverse polities under a single administration; his contribution to legal and administrative procedure was immense. Stoicism's law of nature gave a body to the cosmopolitanism which came to be the official doctrine of the Roman. Man was not a dweller in a particular city (Roman citizenship was early extended to all the inhabitants of Italy and then to the colonies); man was a member of a great common humanity. The state was a natural institution when thought of as world-wide; it was the framework of that great empire which it was the Roman's business to achieve and to administer. And so, in accordance with the law of nature, all discrepancies among the conflicting jurisdictions of particular cities and communities could be adjusted. As a ruler, the Roman believed in justice for all in the performance of duty, in accordance with the law of nature; as an individual in a great engulfing empire, he acquiesced. His individual rights were defined by it. Perhaps, furthermore, there were divinities which could help him; perhaps not. If there were, he was prepared to go along with them; if not, it was not the business of a Stoic to complain of nature.

But before Roman jurists applied Stoic doctrine to the building of a *jus gentium* and justified Rome's entire imperial juristic system in terms of the Stoic *jus naturale*, there appeared both a significant historical analysis of Rome's early success as a republican city-state, and a defense of that earlier simpler polity in those same Stoic terms. Polybius (204-122 B.C.), a Greek hostage in Rome representing the Achaean League, became acquainted with the Roman constitution at first hand and analyzed it in his famous *History of Rome*. He tried to explain the greatness of Rome by tracing its development from the Punic Wars to his own time; the secret of its success to that point he found in the peculiar combination of forces involved in its political set-up. Rome, said Polybius, in Book VI, secured stability by combining the three varying forms of monarchy, aristocracy, and democracy. Each of these was unstable in itself; but, when combined with the others, each played a constructive part. Cyclical changes of governmental forms were avoided. The consuls of republican Rome represented the monarchical principle, the senate the aristocratic one, and the popular assemblies were democratic. Polybius went on to make a clear statement of the check-and-balance theory of government, its first clear statement, in fact; for, while the Athenian writers had expressed some notions of this sort, all of the latter had preferred a form of polity simpler than the complicated mixture praised by Polybius. A brilliant and cogent description of the governmental form of successful, republican Rome resulted, a form which was already changing into the imperial system of later days. The civil wars and Marius, Sulla, Pompey, and Caesar made clear the military way to the imperialism which was to come.

Against the changes that were to identify the power of the people of Rome with the divine right of the god-emperor, Cicero (106-43 B.C.) spoke out as a republican championing the old order. His *De Republica* systematically employed Stoic notions to justify the power of the people and to emphasize that the government was agent of the people in their capacity as state.

Of the simple forms of government Cicero preferred monarchy; the democratic element had got out of hand in Rome and was being exploited by demagogues, he thought. But he defended the existing mixed form as combining the best features of all three types of traditional polity. Cicero's *De Legibus,* as well as the *De Republica,* showed the influence of Plato, but the chief notions are Stoic in character. Civil law must be founded upon the law of nature; justice is conformity to it. Cicero could not know that this natural-law doctrine and its attendant cosmopolitanism were to influence later Roman jurists, as well as to have a revival and a further instructive career fifteen hundred years later; all he in fact accomplished in his immediate setting was to make himself *persona non grata* and insure his own ruin. Imperialism was already on the way in the person of Augustus. To the changes and developments entailed by it, Stoic conceptions offered an ever-ready justification. Practically all the jurists from Seneca to the days of Constantine were Stoics. The *jus naturale* was employed again and again to aid the development of the *jus gentium* and the *jus civile.* It is doubtful whether any other conception, either at this juncture or later, when the doctrine reappears, could have served so well the purposes to which it was put.

Rome had extended her citizenship as no Greek city had done. But this very extension, first to all Italy and later to the whole free population of the Empire, defeated the purposes of self-government. Ultimately anything other than military imperialism became impossible. Power gravitated to the army, and quarrels over the succession sapped the vitality of the Empire. Fighting was a conspicuous cause of ultimate decline. The grandeur that was Rome, bled white by the conflicts of contending generals and their respective armies, became an easy prey to the incoming barbarian.

## CHAPTER IV

## ROMAN CHURCH

While Rome was still in the process of becoming imperial in her official dogma, even while Seneca, with Stoic
austerity, was playing the rôle of mentor to that development, as minister for his monstrous pupil Nero,
there was developing within the Empire a new community which was destined to rise to a controlling position in the future. Indeed, the founder of Christianity
among the Gentiles, the Apostle Paul, is supposed to
have met his death in the persecutions under Nero. The
attitude of this emperor toward the new community of
Christians was brilliantly illustrated by his exploitation
of the effulgent imperial policy of making illuminants of
the communicants. Whatever the conditions under which
the Apostle Paul met his death, it was his enterprise
which made the cult of the early Christians into a Hellenistic religion. From being a dissenting sect of reforming
Jews, with a leader, the "anointed one," who was executed by the authorities, the Christian community broadened into a mystery religion with a full complement of
Hellenistic rites and beliefs.

Like Socrates, Jesus, around whom Christian
dogma centered, left no written record of his teachings; unlike the Greek sage he had no Plato to write
up his doctrine in systematic and literary form. This

left his teaching to be refracted through oral discourse and written down chiefly by those who had not seen him. What he thought and said became tangled with what others thought and said both about him and about his utterances. The early Christians seem to have thought of Jesus as engaged in the work of the expected Jewish Messiah and to have operated in every respect within the ideological framework of the eschatology of late Judaism. The growing strength of their community, and the possibility that the "kingdom" of which they spoke might turn out to be more than a utopian dream, brought them into conflict both with the Jewish cult leaders in Jerusalem, always jealous of their priestly power, and with the Romans, who saw any disturbance as a thing sedulously to be avoided. From the Roman point of view, a group which announced the end of things and a new leader might cause trouble in Palestine; Roman authorities expected that the death of that leader would quell the commotion. But the enthusiastic zeal of the Apostle Paul, who possessed Roman citizenship and used it, spread a body of teaching about Jesus throughout Asia Minor, Greece, and Macedonia which compared favorably, in its popular interest and appeal, with that of any of the other cults of the day. From being a sect of Jews, Christianity became a religion of the Roman Empire, competing with the mysteries of Mithras, of Isis and Serapis, of Atargatis and of the Magna Mater. It outgrew Jewish eschatology almost at once, and absorbed Stoic and

Platonic ideas as its tradition broadened. Politically it was still insignificant, but a chain of centers had been established with Antioch as a base.

The second century saw the philosophic elaboration of the tradition. The author of the Fourth Gospel, Athenagoras, Tertullian, Justyn Martyr, and the writer of the Epistle to Diognetus—the so-called second century apologists—gave coherent philosophical background to Christianity. It became more than a religious mystery, such as other Hellenistic cults; it also became a philosophy. Other popular cults had similar reinterpretation given them, but Christianity received a most thorough recasting. After the second century it continued to compete for popular attention; but it had gained, in addition, an intellectual appeal which compared favorably with Stoicism and Neoplatonism. These latter systems of philosophy lacked the popular appeal which Christianity possessed. In short, the tradition of the Christian community had acquired all the advantages of all its competitors and, in addition, it skillfully exploited the prestige of the whole of ancient Jewish literature. The center of organizing activity shifted again, not back to Jerusalem, the center of the early Palestinian group, but from Antioch to Alexandria; both the extension of the organization and internal strengthening of it progressed. It was no longer a question of quelling a potential riot in a far-off province of the Empire, of prosecuting and persecuting headstrong individuals who occasionally appeared to be agitators against the official Roman religion and its tolerated cults. Christianity became a definite competitor of Rome, with a compact and efficient internal organization. It had come a long way since the primitive Palestinian communistic group had waited for the return of their Messiah and the end of the world.

The Empire tended, therefore, to abandon, in reference to Christianity, its policy of general religious toleration. The Caesars were frightened by the intolerance and aggressiveness of the sect, with its elaborate system of deacons, priests, bishops, and patriarchs. They even supported occasionally some of its competitors, such as Mithraism, which had been popular among the soldiers. Some of the most powerful of the emperors were intensely opposed to Christianity, notably Diocletian. When the abdication of the latter took place in A.D. 305, a persecution of some sixty years duration, initiated by Decius in A.D. 251, drew to an end. The Empire had exerted its full force to eliminate this dangerous *imperium in imperio* and had not been successful. The edicts of persecution were repealed in A.D. 311, and in A.D. 313 Constantine recognized Christianity as one of the legal religions of the Empire. This did not mean that it had the whole field to itself, but that the fight of the Christian community for legal recognition was won. It was only years later, after Julian's attempt of A.D. 361-363 to substitute paganism for Christianity, that Christianity became the exclusive official religion of the Empire. The statue of Serapis at

Alexandria was broken up in A.D. 390, and the temples of other religions were closed and their rituals proscribed by Theodosius I in A.D. 392.

The recognition of Christianity as a legal religion in A.D. 313 was a policy of discretion on the part of Constantine. If other emperors had failed to eliminate the competing organization by force, why not try utilizing it as part of the imperial machinery? Constantine seemingly did his best to employ the Christian organization as a department of state. Instead of executing bishops, he exploited them. He assumed the headship of the hierarchy, although unbaptized, and did not receive that sacrament, if at all, until he reached the end of his life. The price the bishops paid for imperial favor was the acceptance of imperial domination; Constantine called and presided over the Council of Nicaea as an unbaptized pagan. Among the faithful there were many who saw in these developments not the Christianizing of the Empire so much as the paganizing of Christianity. Caesar had become *pontifex maximus*, representative of God on earth. Empire and Church had become one, but that one was the Empire. This was true, at least for the nonce; and, while a major conflict had been resolved, the character of minor conflicts became even more confused. Heretical movements were now political, or might be; and political rebellion might be ecclesiastical. In fact, all conflicts became by definition both. Arianism, Nestorianism, and Donatism are to be interpreted from this point of view.

In the eastern part of the Empire the new synthetic autocracy was a great success. In spite of men like Chrysostom, the process of subordinating the Church by assimilating it to the imperial administration went steadily forward. From here on the relations of Empire and Ecclesia were solved in Constantinople. The docile eastern bishops accepted appointment and dictation by the Emperor. The Byzantine Caesar was in every respect monarch of all he surveyed. The Eastern Orthodox Church emerged under his tutelage.

Very early it became apparent that the bishops of the West were made of sterner stuff. Ambrose of Milan, for example, refused to invest an Arian with an episcopal see although ordered to do so by Valentinian III. The doctrine of the two powers, sacred and secular, each final in its own area, soon emerged as the official position of the Roman bishop in combating the imperial power. The Western Church asserted its independence on sacred matters, thereby breaking with the Greek Church of the East and initiating a thousand years of intermittently acute controversy in the West concerning the relations of the secular and sacred authorities.

Augustine (A.D. 354-430) did not write his famous *City of God (De Civitate Dei)*, primarily to solve this problem, but in it the position of the metropolitan bishop of Rome is clearly set forth. The Emperor, he states, has his authority from God, must be obeyed by his subjects, and should assist in stamping out such

heretics as Donatists and Pelagians. But in sacred matters the authority falls entirely into the hands of the
ecclesiastics.

The writing of the *De Civitate Dei* was occasioned by
the sacking of Rome in A.D. 410 by the Visigoths.
Presumably the writing took place between 412 and 427.
Augustine died in A.D. 430 during the siege of the city
of Hippo by the Vandals. The sack of Rome occurred
eighteen years after the closing of the pagan temples,
and the *pagani* argued that it was a result of the deser-
tion of the old worship. Augustine attacks this, and
argues aggressively that Christianity, if adopted uni-
versally, would save the Empire. Christianity itself is
the City of God in contrast to paganism; this is the
drift of his doctrine in some passages. In others, the
City of God is the Church in contrast to all outside
it; in still other passages it is the community of the
saved. Throughout Augustine's writing it is apparent
that the duality of things impressed him. The time was
out of joint and it was important to be on the right
side. His intellectual development had been very complex; his thought was a peculiar fusion of Christian
tradition, Neoplatonic philosophy, and Roman law. But
the material which he organized had a most extensive
influence on his successors. He articulated a new vision,
albeit a vague one, for a troubled and decaying world.

Things went from bad to worse in the Western Empire. Barbarian kings displaced the Caesars, and the
tie with Constantinople was broken. This crushing of
the secular power by the invaders of the West played

into the hands of the priestly hierarchy—the bishop
of Rome and his subordinates, for the barbarians were
won over to the Christian faith and the integrity of the
Church was substituted for the dissipated hegemony
of the Empire. The fiction was retained that Rome was
one (the whole Middle Ages were haunted by the ghost
of the Empire), but the thread of authority had been
snapped. The old imperial structure centered in Constantinople; only once, under Justinian in the sixth century, was the old unified authority effectively exercised.
But so great was the power of the fiction that it was
preserved, though it was ineffective. Even in the eighth
century, the formal tie to Constantinople still remained;
in Roman theory the Byzantine Emperor was lord of
temporal affairs while in Byzantine theory the Roman
Pope was a provincial bishop. In practice, however, the
Roman Pope hated and feared the Caesar for being an
autocrat in affairs of the Eastern Church, while the
Caesar felt equally sincere in his detestation of the Pope
because of the temporal power which the Roman curia
was actually exercising in the West.

This was the ambiguous situation which Leo III de-
cided to terminate in A.D. 800 by his *coup d'état*, the
coronation of Charles the Great (A.D. 768-814) as Emperor. Leo was not content merely to sever his relations
with the Eastern Empire, but stated that the Empress
Irene was deposed and that the Empire was given to
Charles by him in virtue of his divine authority as suc-
cessor of Peter. Charles was put into a highly embar-
rassing position by Leo's act. He was a powerful king,

but his ideas seem to have gone no further than the dual organization of the secular Empire which had previously obtained. He wanted to be Emperor of the West, and to make arrangements himself to that effect with Irene, whom he once had thought of marrying. What he desired least of all was to accept the imperial designation from Leo. The bold but condescending act of the Pope left the relations of Charles to Irene, and more particularly to Leo himself, in a condition even more ambiguous than before. The stage was set for hundreds of years of conflict and endless debate over spheres of authority and the definition of powers.

The story of the debate is a long one. When a strong emperor was in control of the West the doctrine of the supremacy of the secular power was asserted by him and his apologists; the old tradition of imperial Rome was revived. Such men as Charles and Otto I regarded bishops as minor officials. The doctrine of equality was then put forward by the Bishop of Rome. When at a disadvantage, the best the Pope could hope for was a tolerated equality involving the familiar division of sacred and secular. He rarely got it from a strong emperor, but he always claimed it.

When a strong pope, a Nicholas I or an Innocent III, was in command at Rome and the Emperor was at a disadvantage in the struggle, the classical doctrine of absolute supremacy was applied in turn to the papal office. The Pope appointed and deposed rulers when he could and claimed this power as his Petrine prerogative. He was ably supported by such capable apologists as

Bernard of Clairvaux (A.D. 1091-1153), John of Salisbury (A.D. 1110-1180), Thomas Aquinas (A.D. 1227-1274) and Aegidius Romanus (A.D. 1247-1316). It was then the Emperor's turn to appeal to the doctrine of the two powers and to claim a brotherly equality with the Pope. Needless to say, he did not receive such recognition from a powerful pope, but he always claimed it.

The doctrine of the two powers was essentially a defensive weapon used by a ruler, either ecclesiastical or secular, when he was too weak to maintain the old classical supremacy. When he felt himself strong enough to claim the *suprema potestas, imperium,* or *plenitudo potestatis,* he did it, and denied thereby that anyone was his equal. When two strong men came into control, one in the church and the other in the Empire, a terrific struggle ensued. The contending rulers condemned each other both literally and figuratively while hosts of apologists took up the defense of their respective leaders. Several of these major conflicts, small-sized though chiefly verbal civil wars, developed during the Middle Ages: Gregory VII (Hildebrand) *vs.* Henry IV; Hadrian IV and Alexander III *vs.* Frederick I; Gregory IX and Innocent IV *vs.* Frederick II; and, finally, John XXII *vs.* Louis IV.

The tide of battle ebbed and flowed. After a few early emperors the papal party had the better of the argument. The doctrine of papal supremacy was prevalent on the Continent almost continuously from A.D. 800 to 1300. Sometimes all that even a very powerful emperor

4

could do was to claim equality. He was fortunate when he achieved it. The supporters of secular supremacy were decidedly in the minority up to the very end of the Middle Ages when that doctrine was revived and applied, not to the emperor, but to the rising secular monarch of the modern national state.

Before this took place, however, an attempt was made to settle some of the intolerable ambiguities of the situation by another route. Assuming that the *Respublica Christiana*, which had dominated the scene for some five hundred years, was to continue, what could be done to avoid the internecine struggles which on four occasions had disrupted the peace of all Western Europe? On the occasion of the last great conflict, and during a break in the ecclesiastical ranks occasioned in part by the strategy of the struggle, the program of government by great councils, analogous to earlier ecumenical councils such as that of Nicaea, was suggested. The Conciliar Movement, so-called, was an attempt, albeit an unsuccessful one, to establish responsibility within the structure of the ecclesiastical-political system dominated by the Roman curia. If it had succeeded, the course of subsequent history might have been very different. A reformed and democratized though theocratic Church might have avoided some of the pitfalls of both Reformation and religious wars. Certainly national states would have developed differently. Of course, history always might have been different had events proved otherwise. But the Pope, in this instance, insisted on his superior prerogatives within the Church system and thereby overplayed his hand. The system proceeded to go to pieces in slow but irretrievable fashion.

Social change came slowly in the Middle Ages. The vicious ambiguity of a two-headed system had to be repeatedly demonstrated in four great struggles. But it finally became clear. Men began to see that they were caught between a pontifical Scylla and an imperial Charybdis and that something had to be done. One or the other, perhaps both, had to be eliminated.

## CHAPTER V

## ABSOLUTE MONARCHY

When any social system postulates its own sanctity, supremacy, and inviolability, it is already approaching its end. "Whom the gods would destroy they first make mad." When Boniface VIII rattled the keys of authority so defiantly and exultantly in 1302 (the bull *Unam Sanctam*) the Papacy already had endured almost as long as did the old Roman Empire itself; for five hundred years the Pope had been the absolute skipper of that Ark of Salvation with all Western Europe on board. It was inconceivable to him that it should not go on. But the final storm was approaching and there were breakers ahead.

While the last great medieval conflict was in progress, when John XXII and Louis IV were embroiled, when the Great Schism was at its height and the Conciliar Movement was under way, national differences were beginning to be more operative politically. The national kings were asserting more and more authority. The city-state was developing in Italy and Germany, superior to the ancient city in that it had no slave economy, but having all the factional weakness of its classic predecessor redefined in terms of medieval groupings instead of the family and class groups of ancient Greece. In every respect the situation was becoming more complex.

Did kings have divine right? Who made the law? What was the relation of the common law to the *lex*? Who possessed the right to command? These, and other questions, were being asked not only on the level of Empire and Papacy but also of nation-state and city-state. Aristotle's *Politics* had been introduced into the arena of doctrinal debate by Thomas Aquinas. In most cases the arguments of the various apologists took the form of utilizing classical doctrines of one type or another and of repeating Church fathers and earlier medievalists. Of state theory in the fully modern sense there was none. There was a welter of conflicting allegiances with a veritable dog-fight going on among the leaders for personal ascendancy.

In retrospect it can be seen that the line of development suggested by John of Paris (c. 1300), Peter Dubois (c. 1255-c. 1312) and Marsiglio of Padua (c. 1278-1343) was in fact followed by subsequent events. These men championed the cause of secular territorial kings against the ecclesiastical hierarchy. The *Defensor Pacis* (1324) of Marsiglio sounds almost modern, and his ideas strangely fit the developments of the European scene two hundred years later. With an insight born of knowledge of current events and of ancient experience he demands peace, monarchical rule, a Papacy responsible to all the faithful and minding its own sacred business, and asserts the supremacy of the secular power. It is easy to understand why the Empire rejected his doctrine and the Pope excommunicated its author while indexing his great work.

The Pope and the Emperor continued their age-long conflict, each encouraging insubordination among the followers of the other, to the progressive discrediting of both. The territorial local lords, whose feudal possessions by way of land were contiguous, gradually learned to play one overlord against the other instead of being utilized exclusively for the purposes of their superiors. Steadily they gained in power. Particularly in areas now called Spain, France, and England strong monarchies emerged. Neither Germany nor Italy had been a single feudal *dominium;* petty states of one sort or another appeared in both places. Printing had been invented and was being popularized. Firearms were coming into general use, and soon any man, whatever his origin, would be the military equal of the most noble knight on horseback. Towns were built; commerce developed. Columbus sailed. Copernicus reflected. A new world was in the making. Europe, in fact, did not settle the conflict between Pope and Emperor. It simply outgrew it.

The newness of the situation is excellently reflected in the work of Machiavelli (1469-1527), who did more than anyone else in this early modern period to secularize political thinking. This famous Florentine acted as an official of the Florentine republic for fourteen years prior to the return, in 1512, of the Medici. He did not lack knowledge of the politics of the day. Alexander VI (the Borgia) and Julius II had been on the papal throne; Henry VII ruled in England, Charles VIII (who invaded Italy in 1494) and Louis XII in France,

Ferdinand in Spain, and Maximilian in Germany. Re-
lieved from public office by the incoming of the Medici,
Machiavelli wrote voluminously. His *History of
Florence* is the first history to be written in the modern
manner. His *Art of War, Discourses on Livy*, and *The
Prince* are full of shrewd clear-eyed reflections on political affairs, although, as a minor point, he seems to have
underestimated the military significance of small firearms. He saw that Italy was not becoming unified, as
were Spain and France. He feared absorption of it by
more powerful states. His solution for the problem was
the formation of a strong national Italian state, with
a large militia. Owing to the exigencies of the time, an
unscrupulous autocrat would have to be its ruler.

Actual developments in Italy, of course, did not
follow his wishes. For 350 years the Papacy controlled
central Italy and thwarted all attempts at unification.
But in sketching his theories Machiavelli departed remarkably from the medieval tradition. He does not
quote the *corpus juris civilis*, the *corpus juris canonici*,
or the Church fathers in his writings. Only fifty years before, the *Monarchia* of Rosellinus had been thoroughly
larded with such quotations. The shift toward a consideration of policies in terms of themselves, and their
consequences, is very dramatic. He tried to tell, as he
says, the "truth of things." He did it remarkably well.
He tried to be a realist in political affairs ; when in charge
of the militia in Florence he had hired a notorious
murderer to train the troops. He was strongly republican in sympathy, but became convinced that only a well-

armed tyrant could meet the requirements of the situation. His famous *Prince* was a little book on how a tyrant should conduct himself if he expected to get ahead in the world. He seemingly hoped that one of the Medici might take his advice seriously and become the leader of a united Italy. At all events he sent this famous book to one of them, Lorenzo, probably not intending it for publication but rather for private edification. It is a complete exposé of the art of autocratic government, past, present, and future. It portrays the necessity for practicing systematic deceit, artful hypocrisy, and unscrupulous cruelty if one is to succeed as a prince. The book was published almost immediately and has influenced modern statecraft profoundly. Many a modern autocrat has fulminated against Machiavelli, and denounced his theories, while observing his principles to the letter in actual practice. Indeed, the art of statecraft has not changed materially since Machiavelli. And in his defense let it be added that he did not divorce politics from the moral life. He simply laid down the major premise that the *summum bonum* for a prince is to keep himself in control of the power; and he had the audacity to accept the logical consequences of that assumption. If political ethics and personal morality ever were married, he said in effect, they have been living almost constantly in a state of separation.

Although Machiavelli stated a secular theory of politics, the religious issue was not removed from the arena of discussion. Indeed, as he wrote, the Reformation was getting under way as a practical movement of religious revolt which facilitated the breakdown of the *Respublica Christiana*. The medieval church-state was decaying. All movements against the Papacy, whatever their motives, were political in effect. Whether a lawyer stated a secular philosophy of the state, a prince asserted his own divine independence of Rome, or a rebellious ecclesiastic denied the finality of the Pope's authority on religious matters, from the point of view of the Roman curia it was treason. And it was treated as such.

The tangled character of the motives which led to the disruption of the medieval church-state is illustrated by the wide variety of consequences which became apparent by the end of the sixteenth century as a result of the rebellion. Part of the story can be summed up as Teuton against Latin. The northern European groups were tired of domination and exploitation by southern Europeans. Princes and cities were hostile to the pettifogging Emperor who was dominated by an unscrupulous and corrupt Pope. Those groups which were socially oppressed were glad to rebel against their lords, both civil and ecclesiastical. Those economically dispossessed welcomed the seizure of Church property. The minor clergy were glad to rebel against their corrupt and arrogantly autocratic superiors. Morally the rebellion was a protest against the degeneracy of the ecclesiastical organization. Theologically it was a return to more simple doctrine and a renewed emphasis on personal piety. Intellectually it was a revolt against the tyranny of fixed tradition and made a reassertion of freedom.

It was "individualistic" in every sense of the word. But, whatever the motives which animated the rebels, all their blows fell on Rome, a Rome accused not only of reaction and obscurantism but also of secularity and corruption. All roads had led to Rome and every riot was therefore Roman. In a word, there was civil war throughout the whole of Western Europe, with motives inextricably mixed and the Pope crying treason against all opponents.

The chief strands of positive development were those centering around territorial national political groups. National kings emerged and even set up ecclesiastical groupings within their territories which were in some instances as subservient to them as the Eastern Church had been to the Byzantine Emperor. Where it was expedient for the rising national state to become Protestant, it did so. Protestantism won at that point. Where, as in Spain and France, Protestantism allied itself with anti-patriotic, anti-national, reactionary causes, and Roman Catholicism could and did become nationalistic, the latter remained the popular religious form. Protestantism was suppressed with a fury equaled only by that visited upon Catholics in areas in which they were opposing the national state. The struggle was primarily that of Roman Church-state against rising national states, and the national states won. Roman religion survived chiefly where it adapted itself with sufficient alacrity, where it was not caught in rebellion against the new arbiters of Europe's destiny—the national kings. It was a shift from continental autocratic

theocracy to national secular despotism. Was it a jump
from the frying-pan into the fire? Only the future could
tell.

The amount of civil disorder and intellectual incoherency accompanying such a transition was almost
inconceivable. A veritable wilderness of anarchy,
political, religious, economic, social, ethical, and intellectual developed. In the maelstrom of conflicting interests cross-currents of every sort appeared. Men
might agree on one point, to differ on all others; they
might agree on all points but one, and yet kill each
other with a clear conscience. The most amazing disorder pervaded Western Europe. Similar anarchy accompanied the decay of ancient Rome; but the decay
of medieval Rome was more complex and the story is
better documented for historical insight.

While the same general embroilment between the re-
treating Roman Church-state and the territorial kings
was in progress everywhere in Western Europe with
specific strategies and diverse results, it is notable that
the strategy of conflict appeared within the body of
the developing national states themselves. The higher
nobility, as has been mentioned, had learned the political
game, and the outstanding members were trying to
turn their ancestral feudal *dominium* into an area over
which they should have that absolute power which both
Emperor and Pope had sought. How could they do it?
They had to conciliate and consolidate subordinate
groups at home, to assure themselves of local support.
They had not only to fight the Pope above them, but

also the turbulent nobles below them as well as ambitious emulators abroad. Could they stop the disintegration at the level of the territorial overlord, i.e., hold the power for themselves? This was their problem. Consequently, if the Pope supported their own national nobles against them, they cultivated the middle class and used townsmen and yeomen against the disaffected nobles.

Rome was a highly feudalized church, and the religious developments, although declining in importance, had a peculiarly significant bearing on the realignment which was in the making. Where the national king was strengthened by becoming Protestant, he did so; the Church writers then championed anything which was anti-monarchical—the contract theory of the state, democratic power, or the right of tyrannicide. Where the Church could assimilate the rising national interests within its ecclesiastical organization, and be of use to the king with his new-found powers, as "His Catholic Majesty," it did so; Protestant sects, notably in Spain and France, then became anti-monarchical in their theories and asserted all the above-mentioned doctrines. Protestants, therefore, might be monarchists like Martin Luther (1483-1544), or theocratic republicans like John Calvin (1509-1564), or be primarily interested in the "right of rebellion" like Philippe Duplessis-Mornay in his *Vindiciae Contra Tyrannos* (1579); Roman Catholics displayed the same diversities of political thinking. Calvinists and Jesuits particularly, since they were unpopular sects in various countries, developed doctrines to protect minority "rights." Specifically the question of the relation of sacred to secular, which had been debated so lengthily in the Middle Ages, was revived by the claim that within the hotly-contested domain of the new national state there were various subordinate domains of power over which secular authorities could have no ultimate jurisdiction.

The modern problem of religious toleration developed in this manner. When citizens and communicants had been identical, for the most part there had been no problem, excepting only that of the Jew, and he was damned already. But in the reorientation which took place from 1300 to 1600, the new ecclesiastical alignments did not always follow the new political frontiers. No matter how stiff-necked and arbitrary the new dictatorial monarch might be, there were always religious persons in his kingdom who prided themselves on being more so. And, if pressed too hard by governments, they might follow up their anti-tyrannical doctrines with the dagger of the assassin. Violence was met by violence and the fight went on. Protestants had reason to remember Mary Tudor, Mary of Guise, Philip II and Charles IX, as well as the massacre of St. Bartholomew's Day, 1572. Catholics recalled the murder of Cardinal Beaton and of the Duke of Guise. Patriotism for the nation-state was gradually replacing loyalty to the Roman Church, and it was small wonder that such a transition involved confused motive and much useless violence. Men fought according to their lights, and the illumination was at a minimum.

The problems left by the decay of medieval Rome were not solved in the twinkling of an eye. Indeed, it is fairer to say that they are still in the process of solution. But the anarchy became so intolerable that men gladly turned to authority for relief. Power is always emphasized as the antidote for disorder; and the absolute monarch of the early modern state performed the definite service of reordering the sadly shattered ranks of Western European society. The formula put forward was *secular sovereignty* and *religious toleration*.

Jean Bodin (1530-1596), a professor of law at Toulouse and Advocate of the King at Laon, has the historical credit for inventing the modern doctrine of sovereignty. Faced with the complicated anarchic situation of the religious wars, civil war, and the running controversies between the French king and the jealous nobility, Bodin argued powerfully in his *Heptaplomeres* for a policy of religious toleration. He published *A Method for the Easy Understanding of History* in 1566 and, in 1576, his great work, *Six Books Concerning the State*. On visiting England with the Duc D'Anjou in 1579, he found a poor Latin translation of his work in use at Cambridge and proceeded himself to translate his *Six Books* from French into a Latin version which came out in 1586.

In this work a systematic analysis of social relations is given. Bodin begins with the family, as did Aristotle. This instinctive grouping, which he conceives in patriarchal Roman fashion, together with the other voluntary groups—corporations, communes, colleges—are welded into a state by the force of sovereignty. This force involves the supreme power to command and to secure obedience. A state (*res publica*) is thus created. Sovereignty (*suprema potestas*) is the power to make laws, to declare war and make peace, to grant pardons, and to appoint officers. While Bodin conceives of the sovereign power as subordinate to moral law and to natural law, he does not precisely define these terms; to all intents and purposes the high Roman doctrine of the *suprema potestas* or *imperium*, about which Pope and Emperor had quarreled during the preceding centuries, was applied to the monarch of the modern state. The Church is subordinated to the secular power as completely as with Marsiglio two centuries earlier. Bodin is ambiguous about the power of taxation. Some passages indicate that this power is part of sovereignty, others imply that it belongs to the aggregate of groups composing the state. His immediate successors among the *politiques*, who were generally in favor of religious toleration and secular supremacy, immediately resolved any ambiguity in his doctrines by including this power of taxation within the prerogatives of the sovereign. Thus was formulated the modern classic doctrine of sovereignty.

It is interesting to note, as illustrating the diverse character of differing situations, the political ideas of a minority writer a few years later than Bodin. Johannes Althusius (1557-1638), who was rescued from historical oblivion by Otto von Gierke's study of him, was a German writer living near the Netherlands. Writing his

*Politica methodice digesta* in 1603, he agrees with Bodin in holding that the basis of the state is a collection of the medieval groupings—nobility, clergy, guilds, corporations, towns, assemblies of magistrates—but departs from him in assigning the power of sovereignty to the organized activity of the whole body of society. Sovereignty is the supreme power to do the purpose of the groups which are parts of the state, "defending the spiritual and bodily welfare" of its members; it is limited to this. It may be placed in the hands of a king by a society, but a ruler who seizes it is a tyrant. Tyranny is against divine law. Althusius thus provides a neat justification for the rebellion by the Protestant Dutch against His Catholic Majesty, the King of Spain.

Althusius confined himself almost exclusively to the internal features of a political society; and he stressed the naturalness and the autonomy of the community. A Dutch jurist and writer, Hugo Grotius (1583-1645), was struck by the developing anarchy among the various states of Europe, and addressed himself particularly to the problem of war. Where could one find a sanction applicable to this? When the supreme power no longer belonged to the Emperor, and had in turn escaped the grasp of the Pope, where could a logical foothold be secured for one who wished to argue for decency and humanity in the conduct of international affairs? This Grotius found in the old notion of natural law which had been carried along in tradition and used in a vague way by all medieval writers whatever their more specific sanctions and justifications had been. Others, notably

Francisco Saurez (1548-1617) and Albericus Gentilis (1552-1608), had been emphasizing natural law as a basis for dealing with the increasing international disorders, but Grotius is credited with having put the whole discipline of international relations into its first systematic form. The external relations of sovereign states was the focus of his attention. He has subsequently been referred to as "the founder of international law."

In his great work, *De jure belli et pacis* (1625), Grotius argues that a natural impulse is the basis of human association. This *appetitus societatis*, when developed and matured into an intelligent association of human beings ordering their behavior according to general principles, is the basis of natural law. The needs of such a community become the standard for judging human behavior. Natural law emerges, therefore, from human nature. Its basic proposition is that contracts must be observed. No society can exist if men will not do what they say they will do. Positive law arises out of this, and is made valid by this natural sanction. Men agree to various rules; but at no point do they compromise their original right of self-preservation. War, consequently, may develop between two individuals, between individuals and a state which they are attacking, between a state and individuals whom it attacks, or between states. This last alternative he discusses in detail, as he argues powerfully that men should not cease to be human even though they are at war, and that nothing should be done which might prejudice the possibility of ultimate peace. The influence of Grotius was

5

great; Gustavus Adolphus is reported to have carried his book with him on his campaigns, and its judicious accents are credited with having tempered the wartime policies of even Louis XIV. A systematic intellectual basis had been laid for what Jeremy Bentham afterwards called "international law."

The old debate about the *imperium*, the *suprema potestas* (the term used by Bodin in his Latin version), or the *plenitudo potestatis*, was recast into the discussions of the *puissance souveraine*, or sovereignty. Feudal social usage had changed the scenery since ancient Rome, and modern commercial and agricultural changes were in progress; differing prerogatives were involved. But it was still the question of who gave the orders and who received them, who commanded and who obeyed. All the quarrels over the redefinition of powers and the exercise of prerogatives centered logically in the discussions of sovereignty. As the earlier notions of social authority had been turned inside out and upside down by the circumstances of political conflict and debate, so this new formulation was destined to receive constant restatement and reformulation as the struggles for power and authority continued in the modern state.

A precise formulation of the modern doctrine similar to that of Bodin was given in English by Thomas Hobbes (1588-1679). England witnessed religious and political disorders similar to those of France and the Netherlands. It had its Presbyterians and Dissenters, even its James I, who wrote a defense of the revived but medievally anachronistic notion of the divine right of

kings (*True Law of Free Monarchies*). The Long
Parliament and the execution of Charles I, the success
of Cromwell and the Puritan army, posed the political
problem for Hobbes in the background of civil war. His
*Leviathan,* published in 1651, defines the origin and
nature of the supreme power in such a way as to refute
both divine-right notions and also the claims of those
groups who asserted that there were smaller spheres of
prerogative with which the state could not tamper. As
with Bodin, absolute authority is for Hobbes the antidote for anarchy. Men in a state of nature (thought
of by Hobbes as a perpetual civil war in which the life
of men was "solitary, poore, nasty, bruitish and short")
came together and organized a commonwealth by con-
tracting with each other to put at the disposal of the
sovereign all their various powers. This, for Hobbes,
irrevocable contract was worded by him as follows, "I
Authorise and give up my Right of Governing my selfe,
to this Man, or this Assembly of men, on this condition,
that thou give up thy Right to him, and Authorise all
his Actions in like manner." All power and strength is
conferred on the sovereign, and by "terror thereof" peace
is achieved at home and mutual aid against enemies
abroad. The person carrying this power "is called
SOVERAIGNE, and said to have *Soveraigne Power;*
and every one besides his SUBJECT."

This contract creates the commonwealth, or
"Leviathan" as Hobbes calls it, and makes one person
representative of all, giving that person command of
the resources of all. The sovereign is absolute and ir-

responsible; he dictates the religion of his subjects, to which they are obliged to conform, although God will honor them for whatever beliefs they may hold in private. The sovereign enunciates all law; the king's reason, properly advised by his ministers, Hobbes declared to be the *summa ratio* and the *anima legis* in England. He thereby championed the emerging function of legislation in opposition to common law procedures. In his notions that man is not fit for society by nature, but must be prepared by education, and that intelligence should be available to deal with emergencies as they arose, on a basis other than mere custom, Hobbes outlined ideas which were developed significantly in later generations. The king gave way to Parliament in the English system, "the king in Parliament," as the phrase goes, and judicial review of legislation has played no significant part in English constitutional development.

The keynote to the political writings of Hobbes, occasioned as he says by the disorders of the times, was peace. Peace had become so important as a means to a tolerable life that even permanent dictatorship was welcomed as a relief. And all men were subjects, all men as individuals. No medieval groupings were recognized by Hobbes, for these groups in their claim of private prerogatives and domains of authority constituted the essence of anarchy in his opinion. They were vermiculate bodies within the great Leviathan which merely made it sick. Hobbes disliked the Presbyterian clergy who meddled in the affairs of the Long Parliament as much as he did the "Papists"; in fact, all intermediate forms of association were deliberately excluded by him.

It is interesting that from here on in English and French thinking the medieval groupings progressively disappear, although they survive in German thinking, where no strong state appeared, to merge later into the collectivistic developments of the nineteenth century. The old groups and estates had proved to be impediments to the free and effective action which the nation-state needed in securing internal harmony. It was the state, the estate of the king, and that alone which could serve the purposes of peace; Hobbes illustrated the drift of development excellently by his exaggerated disregard and contemptuous disapproval of all intermediate forms of association. The fight of the national king against subordinate rebellious nobles was carried out to the conclusion of complete destruction of every medieval prerogative. All men became "subjects" or "citizens," and every group and individual right came to depend, in theory, upon the state for its existence.

Hobbes went to Paris even before the exiled royalists; but the ecclesiastics who took refuge there with Charles howled in holy horror at the Erastianism of his doctrine. They accused him of "atheism." He became *persona non grata* to such an extent that he returned to England and made his peace with Cromwell. He lived through the Restoration almost to the time of the Peaceful Revolution; lacking less than a decade his life spanned those epic English years from the Spanish Armada to the constitutional monarchy of 1688.

## CHAPTER VI

## DEMOCRACY

Hobbes provided an English statement of Bodin's doctrine of sovereignty, basing it on contract and insisting upon the complete subordination of "the sacred" to "the secular." In theory a complete refutation of the papal writings of the thirteenth century had been made. In practice the absolute theocratic continental system of the great popes had given way in Western Europe to the absolute secular supremacy of the territorial national kings. Papacy and the Holy Roman Empire continued; but both, so far as their political significance was concerned, increasingly passed into that limbo of mythical historical potencies already occupied so majestically by ancient Greece and Rome. All the live issues centered around the person of the sovereign monarch of the national state.

It had ever been the fate of men in Western Europe to substitute one monstrous form of government for another. Autocratic Roman emperors had been displaced by designing and corrupt popes, and the latter had given way in turn to equally tyrannical secular despots. There is a poison in power, as has been well said, and the proper antidote seems not to be the futile substitution of one poisonous tyranny for another. Autocrats have been perennially afflicted with inability to distinguish a country's welfare from their own personal well-being. Where theological justifications have been involved (and it must be remembered that all medieval and almost all modern political thinking up to this point saw a holy office in every lordship), the seasoned autocrat came easily and almost inevitably to the clear and distinct logical position that his own personal interests both were and should be supreme by divine right.

The difficulty with social omnipotence in every domain, in short, is that it never has been equipped with even a tolerable degree of the correlative omniscience. Dictatorship has been in fact a counsel of desperation. It has come in response to disorder and anarchy. It has played its part by preserving or restoring a minimum of order in such a situation. The popularity of auto-cratic government in European history consequently may be regarded as an index of the degree to which the whole history of that unfortunate continent has been one desperate emergency after another. No one can deny that the secular monarch performed the service of organizing the modern state. But when all its modest virtues are recognized, it still must be said that if dic-tatorship be institutionalized it decays. It ends by generating an anarchy which may be even worse than that which it was designed to prevent. Indeed, it might be argued that the systematic chronic misgovernment of Europe has been the effective factor in making its his-tory one long unending emergency.

However that may be, the outlines of the modern na-tional states were no sooner defined than the need for internal responsibility became apparent. In England, for example, Tudor autocracy decayed into Stuart tyranny. The need for organizing some tolerable measure of responsibility, which had been felt earlier in England and to which the Conciliar Movement on the continent had been a futile response in the heyday of the Roman Church-State, reappeared in the smaller setting of the national monarchy. How could the sovereign power be restricted in operation so as to perform only in ways which were sufficiently tolerable to hold the allegiance of the subjects of that sovereignty?

Historically major political alterations of a society usually have been accompanied by violence, sometimes so great as to occasion the eclipse of a civilization. Crystallized social and political structures have had to be fused in the melting-pot of great social conflagrations before major reorientations have taken place. Pre-scientific men confronted their social problems as blindly as they did those of hygiene; they perished in civil war, and of bubonic plague and other physical ailments, with equally bovine stupidity. Charles I paid with his life for his inability to make concessions, as did Louis XVI more than a century later. The postulation of absolute authority and infallibility again had been a symptom of decay. The absolute monarch was about to go the way of the absolute Pope while the men of Western Europe muddled through to more responsible forms of national government with an accompaniment of regrettable bloodshed.

The issue involved was clearly seen in Holland by

Benedict Spinoza (1632-1677). In his *Tractatus Theologico-Politicus* (1670) and *Tractatus Politicus* (1677) he displays clearly the influence of Hobbes, but argues that it is as necessary to protect men from those ruling as from those ruled. Human nature is uniform, and it is gratuitous to assume better motives in those who are ruling than in the general population. The ineptitude of the public arises from the fact that they are kept in ignorance of public affairs. The state must rest on the united power of the community of individuals coöperating in free union to secure and further the development of those natural aptitudes from which it takes its rise. Freedom of thought, speech, and religion are essential to the full development of peaceful community life. In suppressing these a state would defeat its own aim and produce only a peace of desolation, barbarism, and slavery. While the *Tractatus Politicus* was unfinished, and published posthumously, it is clear that Spinoza held that civilized and enlightened men should seek a constitutional republican form of government guaranteeing complete religious toleration as part of a wide area of individual liberty.

Protests against the arbitrary exercise of power by the monarch of a nation-state first became effective in England. That country earned the title of "mother of Parliaments" by virtue of its early and dramatic leadership in the development of constitutional limitations. Continental ideas of responsibility had been present in the Conciliar Movement, perhaps even the notion of representative government in the strict sense, but the machinery of its organization had never reached the seats of power as it had in England. And within one hundred and fifty years of the discovery of America the rising seafaring and commercial middle classes of England had so far developed their needs and extended their demands as to insist upon more direct participation in the command of social affairs. They came to feel that the duty of subjection might be overdone, that all command and no obedience on one side and all obedience and no command on the other resulted in an unfair distribution of the goods and services of life. The most restless or footloose might emigrate to the colonies, but those who were tied by responsibilities remained to change their government further to their own liking. The Peaceful Revolution of 1688 represented the triumph of the rising middle class. William and Mary became King and Queen *by act of Parliament*, and a limited monarchy (destined to be more permanent than that of 1399-1461) emerged from fifty years of turbulent disorder.

John Locke (1632-1704) was the spokesman of this English Revolution. He both justified the right of the people to rebel and remake their government in 1688 and also by his doctrines anticipated the coming economic changes. He was to be the authority most quoted by middle-class writers and speakers, English, Continental, and American, for generations to come. His viewpoint represented the landed owner, the industrialist, the people who had gained wealth in the exercise of some employment and who felt that they deserved protection by society in the enjoyment of their property.

Locke's *Two Treatises on Civil Government* (1690), after disposing of the doctrine of the divine right of kings, proceeded to develop a theory of limited monarchy. Throughout the work the word "sovereignty" was avoided and no mention was made of Hobbes. The ideas of the latter were modified one by one in the direction of limiting the supreme power rather than extending it. Locke was not interested primarily in civil peace; that had been achieved. Property did interest him; and the protection of subjects in the enjoyment of their property he conceived to be the first duty of government. The "state of nature" was changed by him from a condition of war to one of peace and industry. The contract, which Hobbes had thought of as irrevocable and between subjects only, not binding on rulers, Locke used as a double one, first between subjects and then between them and the government, binding upon the latter and revocable by the former. In every respect the modifications were in the direction of popular government. The subject, said Locke, gives himself into the power of a "majority" of his fellows, but the power of any and all government is limited by the fact that only part of the subject's natural right is relinquished by him. Property is possessed by the individual before he becomes a subject of any political society; indeed, it is for the purpose of protecting themselves in the enjoyment of property that subjects form a political society. The inconveniences of a state of nature, absence of a known law, of an impartial judge, and of an administration to enforce decisions,

lead men to organize the commonwealth. Consequently
no government of the commonwealth can take the property of subjects from them without their consent. Should
any government do this, it would be violating the purpose
for which it was designed. The subjects had mixed their
labor with the objects of nature, and thereby, subject
to limitations of use, had made natural objects their
own; furthermore, they had established by consent the
convention of money, an imperishable metallic form of
property. The business of the commonwealth was to
protect them in the enjoyment of their properties in
peace and safety.

An organized civil society is therefore a commonwealth which provides the things wanting to man in the
state of nature: the legislature which provides the law,
the judges to settle disputes under the law, and execu-
tives to enforce the law. Property rights remain natural; so does the right of worship. The commonwealth
must adopt a policy of toleration in religion, so long as
its existence is not thereby compromised (*Letters on
Toleration*). So ran the liberal philosophy of Locke,
and all his ideas were of immense historical significance
both in Europe and in the United States of America.

While English autocrats were fighting a losing battle
against the rising middle class, both in theory and in
practice, on the continent, in practice at least, autocracy kept the advantage. Liberal Frenchmen admired
the English developments and praised England's constitution, notably Montesquieu (1689-1755). Although
he had visited England in person, his *Spirit of the Laws*

(1748) described the English state largely through the eyes of Locke's second treatise. He emphasized the tripartite division of powers. But Locke's "legislative, executive and federative" were metamorphosed into an equally Polybian "legislative, executive and judicial" by Montesquieu. In this form the doctrine was widely influential and affected not only European thinkers and statesmen but also the framers of the Constitution of the United States. Although Montesquieu, like Machiavelli, stood outside the main stream of development, his writing, even as that of the great Florentine, took subtle effect upon subsequent events.

The notion of sovereignty, and political ideas in general, received still further and more drastic emendation at the hands of Rousseau (1712-1788). His great work, *The Social Contract* (1762), was the chief source of the philosophy for the French Revolution. Legend has it that Robespierre read it once a day that he might not forget. Sovereignty, said Rousseau, is the rightful power of the majority. He went on to develop a systematic justification of popular supremacy. The idea of a state of nature was employed, again slightly changed, as a background for a contract theory of the state. In a state of nature man had been in a desirable pleasant condition, according to Rousseau, and the history of society displayed a deterioration of his wellbeing. Man became enslaved by tyrants. Rightful social power was that possessed by the "common will," which resulted when men organized themselves into a state by means of the contract: "Each of us puts in common his person and his whole power under the supreme direction of the general will; and in return we receive every member as an individual part of the whole."

This contract was effective among citizens only; they, as sovereign, in their legislative deliberations voiced the law which they were bound to obey as people. The government was composed merely of the officials who were designated to enforce those laws and were not at all, as Hobbes had said, in possession of the power of the state. That power remained theoretically resident in the common will, of which the executive officer, or officers, were servants. And Rousseau pointed his finger at the whole corrupt French monarchy when he wrote (Bk. III, Ch. X), "So that as soon as the government usurps the sovereignty, the social compact is broken, and all the ordinary citizens, rightfully regaining their natural liberty, are forced, but not morally bound, to obey."

The *suprema potestas* had come a long way since Pope and Emperor had wrangled over it. The Pope had lost it to the absolute monarch of the early modern state. The latter had been limited in its use by the beginnings of the constitutional movement. Now it was attributed in theory by Rousseau to the people only, as a power inalienable and supreme, indivisible and sacred. The common will was always right; it commanded all property and persons. It could force a man to the realization, if not the enjoyment, of his own freedom. In Rousseau we have absolutism, but popular absolutism. With Hobbes, and *contra* Locke, all intermediate forms of association and "rights" were disregarded. They were the essence of anarchy. The problem of a just state was solved, not by limiting and impeding the executive through inalienable natural rights which were by definition extra-political in character, but by the complete subordination of everyone and everything to the pure democracy of popular control. Even representative government was discounted; the people of England were asserted by Rousseau to be free, in fact, only occasionally, namely, while they were voting for their representatives. Afterwards they were enslaved. Rousseau envisaged, instead of a representative system, a glorified town-meeting type of political set-up, an Athens resurrected, or his own Geneva. Economic and political factors were combined, with the former definitely subordinated to the latter. At this point Rousseau became the inspiration of subsequent socialism and communism.

Dunning has remarked (*Political Theories*, Vol. III) that every possible form of political theory had been suggested by the end of the Greek period. The same might be said of the modern period from 1300 to 1800. The complete gamut from continental theocratic autocracy to pure democracy had been completed in theory by 1762.

The historical importance of Rousseau in political thinking was tremendous. Every traditional influence moved into his thought and every subsequent political writer was influenced by him. He introduced ethical and psychological ideas (right and will) into the arena of political thought and yet continued to employ the juristic and metaphysical notions (contract, nature) which had been stressed previously. In social philosophy his work is comparable in significance to the pivotal position of Kant in the history of modern logic and metaphysics.

The notions of contract and nature had an instructive career. The former dates from the Sophists in Greece (law *vs.* nature), was mentioned by Lucretius in his *De Rerum Natura,* and was revived by modern thinkers to be utilized in various ways, either among individuals who theoretically divest themselves of power and give it to the sovereign as with Hobbes, or in a double form as with Locke, or by a different single contract organizing the sovereign common will of Rousseau. The history of the notion is illustrative of the various uses to which a single legal idea can be put in social thinking, given the diverse situations of time and circumstances which history presents. The idea of nature had a similarly enlightening career. As old as Greece, and as familiar as contract, it was employed in equally diverse ways. The state of nature was evil, a state of civil war, with Hobbes; it was "inconvenient," but a condition involving certain natural, even divine, uses and freedom, according to Locke. With Rousseau it was good; and its glories could be recovered only by that perfect state which appeared when a proper common will was formed. Men were noble savages, real individuals in nature, Rousseau thought; in most existing states man was neither an individual nor a citizen, but he could

become a citizen and gain his morality and culture
without accepting slavery, if the just rule of the common
will were supreme. Both with the notion of contract and
that of nature it was apparent that what political
thinkers desired was a basis of criticism, a standard of
judgment by which they could articulate their criticisms
of current societies. They employed the logical materials
which lay at hand, utilizing them in differing ways as
lumber to construct the various logical edifices which
their purposes prescribed. All pre-scientific political
thinking proceeded in an atmosphere of logical con-
demnation and justification in which such notions were
peculiarly fertile.

Adverse criticism of Rousseau, as of every political thinker, is easy, but largely futile. The significance
of the man is not in his logic, but in the forces he
released, the needs and urgencies which he voiced. If
it be said that no omnipotent autocrat, ecclesiastical
or secular, ever has possessed the requisite correlative
omniscience, it is equally true, with reference to democratic theory, that no omnipotent majority ever has
possessed that omniscience. Ignorance has been the
perennial vice of the accredited leaders of humanity,
be they one, few, or many. No form of government,
just as no social class, ever has possessed a monopoly
of stupidity. As regards Rousseau, one cannot condemn
a thinker for not defending the rights of minorities
against majorities, when the primary rights of the
latter had not been achieved. Majority rule had to
appear above the horizon before its shadows could be

perceived. The demand for democracy arose simply as a result of the intolerable inflexibility of other forms. No one could know what those who were governed wanted, to have and to avoid, so well as they themselves. How they could achieve their ends, even assuming them to be definable, might prove an enigma in any pre-scientific age.

## CHAPTER VII

# NATION-STATE

The early modern national state, as we have recounted, developed from the *dominium* of the powerful feudal lord. As a division of the *Respublica Christiana,* it had functioned for the most part as a subordinate administrative area. But the aggressive feudal lords of Western Europe denied the superior jurisdiction of the Pope, refused to tolerate the subordinate groupings of medieval society, and emerged as absolute sovereigns of nations of individual subjects. The subjects then proceeded to limit the powers of these monarchs in turn and, finally, in democratic theory, defined sovereignty in more recent modern theory as the proper quality of their own collective activity.

Accompanying this change from a feudal administrative area to a modern territorial national state, there apeared an increasing amount of conflict. The rulers of each state claimed the absolute authority formerly held only by Pope oᵣ Emperor. In effect, the kings of Spain, France, and England developed into miniature emperors after the ancient Roman pattern, commanding the allegiance, and devotion to death, of their subjects. Even where and when monarchy disappeared, as in the French Revolution, or in America, the nation-state continued to command this allegiance. Authority shifted from Papacy to monarchy, and then from

monarchy to nation-state. The latter shift was as
significant as the former and developed progressively
out of it. The fabric of feudal society gradually was
unraveled and rewoven in terms of nationality. Nationalism supplanted religion; it became a history, a career,
a destiny. The feudal administrative area, so to speak,
passed through the stage of absolute monarchy and
emerged in theory as an organization not only having
the juristic attribute of sovereignty and a certain
geography and climate, as Montesquieu suggested, but
also possessing the economic interests, honor, and
prestige of a human personality with a will.

Rousseau's idea of the common will had much to do
with this; out of it a vague pre-scientific social psychology appeared, the German notion of the *Volkgeist*,
and the metaphysical idealism of that country. The idea
came into vogue that collectivities of action had certain
involuntary psychic emanations which constituted their
distinctive cultures. If we add racial continuity, as the
idea of a "nation" appeared in the writings of such men
as J. G. Herder (1744-1803), we get most of the factors
which were involved in the political philosophy of the
nineteenth century. Nationalism became in theory a
biology, a psychology, a history, and a metaphysics, as
it provided more and more definitely the basis of political
motivation. Personal allegiance to a sovereign monarch
passed through participation in the "common will" and
became loyalty to a nationality which implemented the
individual in all the functions of his life.

Many of the elements which coalesced around the turn

of the century to accentuate the occurrence we call national consciousness had been gradually developing for many generations. Language, literature, economic life, legal institutions, those disparities of custom and tradition which constitute the cultural nationality of a group, whether or not identified with a specific political organization, can be traced in their beginnings in some instances as far back as the ninth century. National sentiment gradually increased. It had been used in England by Henry VIII and Elizabeth and even before that. But, around 1800, the study of history brought it into focus as more and more significant. The resulting idea of cultural nationality, such as that of Herder, need not have become a political concept in the narrow sense of the word. In Herder's thought it was combined with political cosmopolitanism.

This notion of cultural nationality had been latent in Rousseau. Indeed, the influence of Rousseau was the primary force which led the German writers to idealize *Kultur* as contrasted to nature. Culture for him had been the body of institutions which natural man acquired as he became civilized. Rousseau had tended systematically to discount civilization and to idealize natural man, the "noble savage." The "common will" had been a refuge for him from that decadent culture which contemporary society exhibited; it was a goal which might be achieved by a truly just society. Herder shifted the emphasis; cultural, institutional factors were stressed by him as important, as having continuous development, as constituting cultural nationality. The development of the historical study of language and literature made this shift easy and tended to enhance the consciousness of these as national products. It remained to emphasize historical study of other factors in cultural nationality and to fuse the latter notion with the political idea of the "common will" (both deriving from Rousseau), and national political consciousness as it appeared in the nineteenth century assumed more definite form.

Immanuel Kant (1724-1804) was not the thinker who effected the junction of all these ideological factors, but his influence was very great. In his thinking the rational (civilized) man gained further in prestige as contrasted to the natural man of Rousseau. Kant treated history as a process of the gradual subjugation of the natural by the rational, and the state figured in the drama as facilitating the process. The moral and rational nature of man was helped by the external force of the state in the progressive realizing of the ideal moral law. This latter involved the principle that the freedom of each shall be reciprocal with the freedom of every other. Kant went on to affirm that the state in turn was to be facilitated in its development by the idea of a world state, and of international law, which came in to help the various states organize into a peaceful human society (*The Philosophy of Law* and *Project for a Perpetual Peace*).

Kant was cosmopolitan, humanitarian, even democratic and international, as other eighteenth century writers had been, but in his thinking, culture, or civilization, became more closely allied to the morally excellent and the rational. The "affections" of the noble savage of Rousseau became but raw materials, no longer ideal, out of which a moral order might be made by a historic process. This process would unveil a regular movement, a slow but constant progressive development of the primordial dispositions of humanity.

This historical process J. G. Fichte (1762-1814) attempted to describe more fully (*Characteristics of the Present Age*) as involving five stages of which the contemporary age was the third. In this third period the state operated as a constraining institution having the purpose of producing moral ideals out of natural egotism. The state, said Fichte, is an "artistic institution"; its purpose is culture. It is a means to the realization of the entire capacities of the individual; and when these are realized, *Kultur* is the result. This state is the vocation of mankind.

Thus, in Fichte's mind, the juristic notion of the state fused with that of cultural nationality. The state was to further culture, even when distant barbarians across the seas were being subjugated. Unconsciously its activities helped the inevitable process involved.

The thinking of Fichte is very important to the development of nineteenth-century European nationalism. In his early period he followed Rousseau in talking about the law of nature, rights of individuals, and sovereignty of the people, while his later writings emphasized the national state, even justifying its extension into a state socialism. His *Addresses to the German*

*Nation* (1807-1808) indicated a shift from cosmopolitanism to nationalism. He championed the purity of the
German nationality; all the German language is "pure
German." Germans, he said, have a folk life, but not a
political life. This latter they must achieve by an act of
sheer conscious will. Upon their success in this depends
the fate of Europe and of civilized man. Fichte's *Closed
Commercial State* expressed the ideal of an economic
life as self-enclosed as the legal area of the political
state had been prior to this time. The state must assume
a protecting attitude toward the economic life within
its borders. Instead of the individualistic *liberté* of Rousseau, which Kant had tended to use in his political
thinking, Fichte emphasized more and more such ideas
of Rousseau as involved the supremacy of the state.
Such passages as the famous dictum of Rousseau that
a man can be "forced to be free" became the center of
his thought. Militant patriotism became a moral duty.
The chief factor in this shift was probably the
Napoleonic wars. Fichte sympathized with the early
struggles of the French republic, but, in reaction to
Napoleon, nationalism became, in his thinking, something more than it ever had been before. Religion had
been involved in political questions of the day since the
Middle Ages; but now language, race, law, literature,
industry, and all other cultural developments seemed
to be at stake along with the political administrative
organization. The cult of the nation-state was emerging
with a metaphysical drama comparable to the Drama
of Salvation.

The thinker who stated the new idealistic philosophy of nationalism in its most categorical form was G. W. F. Hegel (1770-1831), who succeeded Fichte as professor of philosophy at the University of Berlin. Hegel believed, with both Kant and Fichte, that the fundamental essence of all nature was mind; hence the name idealism. Nature as a whole had become assimilated to the common will, thought of as developing by internal rather than external causal factors. Will and mind had become metaphysical principles. All development, all history, was described by Hegel in terms of the imminent dialectic in accordance with which this rational principle unfolded. The nationalism which Fichte sketched in tentative form, yet to be realized as an actual achievement, was stated by Hegel and his followers as a metaphysical dogma.

Hegel's logic involved the famous formula, *thesis*, *antithesis*, and *synthesis*. Every reality, said the theory, was negated by a contradictory, only to emerge into a higher fusion of the two previous contradictories. Progress takes place by virtue of this constant internal pendulum swing in which opposition is overcome and a new truth achieved on a higher level. This logical formula Hegel applied to the universe, assuming it to be the key to reality as a whole (*Philosophy of Law, Philosophy of History*). He not only saw in his own philosophy a synthesis of the opposition of eighteenth-century rationalism, on one side, and of romanticism with its emphasis on experience, on the other, but he employed his formula in accounting for the development of all cultural and political forms. History was the dialectic of states. In war they came into conflict; out of it, forming a new synthesis, emerges the victor. This is the rational order of things. The actual is rational and the rational is actual. The ideal will always be embodied. Politically it objectifies itself first in law, then in personal morality, and subsequently in social morality. Finally there appears the political morality of the state, thought of as the ideal, progressively manifesting itself. The state Hegel characterizes in an exuberant passage as "the march of God in the world." The making of constitutional monarchy was not an invention of the modern mind but merely a realization of the divine state which already existed. It was absolute; in it (following Rousseau) the will of each citizen and the common will of the community are fused. In this state only does the individual achieve his freedom, and then only by subordination to it does he implement his life. The imperfect character of the revelation of the ideal causes other and more adequate states to come to ascendancy. War is the process by which the new abode of the absolute will and mind exhibits itself. The nation which has been abandoned has no rights. War makes short work of the stagnation which peace brings to a society. In it the state is obeying its moral law, which is to support and extend itself. Hegel explains that the Teutonic people are the abode of the world spirit in his day, that they have overcome the dualism of the Latin mind and have achieved a new unity. "The pure inwardness of the Germanic soul was the soil of the en-

lightenment of man." Thus were the formal legal notion
of Bodin and Hobbes, and the ethical and psychological
concepts of Rousseau filled in by the metaphysical doctrines of German idealistic philosophy. The national state
emerged as the embodiment of Absolute Reason, of the
Ideal. Rousseau's common will, made into a metaphysical substance, was given the content of his "civilization" (*Kultur*) and was assumed by the Germans in
their thinking as logically prior to his concept of the
natural man. As has been aptly said, the revolutionary
was slain by his own picked weapons.

German Idealism was the dominant philosophy of
the nineteenth century. It is not a figure of speech to
say that nationalism had become the new focus of the
culture of the occidental world. The cult of the Virgin
had been displaced by the cult of the nation-state. The
intensity with which this new organization was achieved
can be understood only when one appreciates the significance of the  work of men like Savigny in historical
jurisprudence, of the Grimm brothers, and of Wolf in
philology, as well as of the Hegelians. Art, religion, and
every strand of cultural life came in for study. The
historical method was applied to all institutions with a
strong emphasis on nationality as the general motif.
The cosmopolitanism of the eighteenth-century intellectual classes gave way to nationalism in the nineteenth
century. As has been observed, this historical study,
even the subsequent psychology of the *Volkseele* and
the notion that ideas arise out of corporate activity,
need not have become organized on the level of political

ideas at all. But throughout the nineteenth century they did this, and the intensification of national consciousness was one of the outstanding features of the intellectual life of that century.

Indeed, the major premise of every important political thinker of the nineteenth century was the assumption, consciously or unconsciously, of the outstanding importance of national groupings, if only, as with anarchists, for purposes of attack. Even the tenacious traditions of individualism, holding over from the days when men had to vindicate their well-being as men against autocratic predatory rulers, gave way gradually to the emphasis on the national groups. The disintegration which had begun with the fourteenth century, and had resulted in such anarchy in Europe as to occasion an overwhelming demand for monarchical dictatorships as a remedy, was reversing itself. A new integration was in the making. Individualistic notions of natural rights, and all the intellectual paraphernalia of the struggle to secure responsibility within those dictatorships when established, tended to grow thin when more national and less personally autocratic forms of government came into being. The new collectivity was the nation, and an augmentation of the functions of the nation state proceeded apace. State structures were developed in practice and justified in theory with an assiduity reminiscent of the organizing of those previous great European political forms, the Greek city-state, the Roman Empire, and the Roman Papacy. Nationality was the new faith, and the patriot was the new saint.

Power gravitated into the hands of the rulers of the national states with increasing rapidity. Wilhelm von Humboldt (1767-1835), who theoretically held, following 1790, that the state could not be trusted to handle education, became, after the turn of the century, one of the founders of the Prussian system of education. The national state was not only the symbol of the conservation of all historical cultural values, but, as an instrument for getting things done, it was almost alone in the field. The old collectivity had been the Roman Church; the new collectivity was the nation-state. And Europe was to follow through the logic of this new orientation to a most bitter end.

But before the defects of the philosophy of nationalism were to be glaringly illustrated, the nation-state had a longer career ahead of it. Nationalism represented an ideal interest, an attachment to a larger and more inclusive goal, throughout most of the nineteenth century. Men differed as regards details of their theories; ideas were as various as the diverse situations in which men found themselves. They argued against each other with vigor and cogency; they fought each other both logically and physically. But out of the tumult and the shouting, above the cloud of conflict of immediate purposes and programs, stronger and clearer, there emerged the nation-state as the ultimate constituent political unit of occidental society.

Guiseppe Mazzini (1805-1872) stated the principle of nationality with religious fervor. He felt the influence of the individualistic natural-rights doctrine of the

previous century and reacted against it. The French
Revolution closed a definite period in history, according
to Mazzini. Its philosophy had been analytic, individualistic, a philosophy of "rights" emphasizing self-interest.
It had been a philosophy of economic advantage. The
new philosophy was to emphasize a synthetic view which
should stress association, the duties of man, social
solidarity, political rather than economic interest. It
should be humanitarian rather than cosmopolitan. A
definite collective life is present in the various nationalities; humanity is an association of nationalities. The
development and coöperation of these nationalities was
the goal to be sought, and Italy was to be the leader
in the nineteenth century. Mazzini's great slogan was
"God and the People." The cultural advance of all
peoples was to be achieved by and through the
predestined division of labor involved in the national
divisions of Europe. Mazzini was almost Hegelian in
his emphasis on nationalism, but he adds the principle
of fraternal coöperation among the various peoples.
Theoretically he represents the way in which the
pantheism of the early nineteenth century took effect
upon political thinking, suffusing the principle of
nationality with a divine and mystic glow. Practically
Mazzini was a politician who plotted against Austria
and wanted a republican unified Italy. He was unsuccessful, but his ideas indicate the way in which the political
tides were running. Nationalism furnished the chief
motif for both the cult of authority and the cult of
revolution, even as in the days of John XXII the as-

sumption of the Church Universal, the Ark of Salvation, had been the preface of all the arguments, both of the autocrats and of the champions of responsibility.

Particularly in those areas in which as yet nationality as a political fact had been unachieved the philosophy of nationality became conspicuously prominent. Germany and Italy were still geographical terms; no more fervent nationalism ever has been written than some of the works of Fichte, Hegel, and Mazzini. In central Europe, for the most part, political unity as a nation-state was still to be achieved. But, both in terms of what had been accomplished and of what was thought of as desirable, there had been a reaction against the extreme individualistic theories of the French Revolution. Edmund Burke (1729-1797), in England, had condemned the activities of the Revolutionists as destructive of all the ancient glories of France. And, when the storm of the Napoleonic Era had passed, practically all thinkers had written of the anarchy of the Revolution either to condemn it roundly as utterly futile or to indicate it as a destructive but necessary phase of social development. The vagaries of the revolutionists made it easy to disregard any virtues inherent in the revolutionary philosophy.

The French writers, De Bonald (1754-1840) and De Maistre (1754-1821), represented another type of reaction to the cosmopolitan individualism of the eighteenth century. Their revival of the traditional Roman Catholic point of view emphasized "sociocracy," by which was meant a religious state socialism. De

Bonald reversed the eighteenth-century doctrine of reason. Reason did not produce truth, said he; truth produced reason. Reason must rest on a revelation, a truth given by God originally, through the gift of speech to man, and handed down as Scriptures. Reason can make nothing; it can only explicate the meaning of those revealed fundamental truths upon which the very existence of organized society depends. Not individual insight or intuition, but collective truth is the amalgam of society. Indeed, the principle of individual judgment has been the cause of all the destructive social developments since 1521. The French Revolution, said De Bonald, was a necessary consequence of the Reformation and of the loss of the proper subordination of the individual to the group. Altruism, which is essential to religion, must be produced by religious education. The failure to subordinate the individual resulted in the anarchy of both Calvinism and democracy. Collective judgment, embodying a truth of authority and religion, is essential to society and to a proper relation in society of "cause, means and effects." De Bonald wrote his philosophy around these last three words, interpreting various institutions in terms of them (e.g., father, mother and children; or, sovereign, ministers and subjects), as well as world history, much after the fashion of Hegel and his "thesis, antithesis, and synthesis." What is new in the position is that religious revelation is made the core of social life. The state must cooperate with the religious orders to ensure the education of its citizens, for without the spiritual power there can be no loyal citizens. The philosophy of the *Respublica Christiana* thus was written down into the nation-state and the primacy of the spiritual power reasserted in this novel way.

De Maistre assumed an equally derogatory attitude toward human intelligence. According to him it is not the conscious but the unconscious elements which are divine. Deliberately man can create nothing. Human reason is merely a diabolically complicating factor in history. All attempts deliberately to write constitutions and to legislate are futile. All such written documents cost more than they are worth. A constitution is simply the statement of the customs which obtain in an area and these have grown up unconsciously. Indeed, history is more rational than reason since it is guided directly by God. De Maistre pressed his position to the point of saying that the existing institutions are divine to the degree that conscious direction is absent, and that the French Revolution was a visitation of divine wrath upon men for setting up human reason against divine authority.

The positive philosophy of Auguste Comte (1798-1857) also reacted against the individualism of the previous century, although Comte regarded the Revolution as neither the evidence of divine wrath nor the work of the devil. Following the philosophy of history of his teacher, Saint-Simon (1760-1825), he held rather that it represented a vast negative phase of historical development, destructive but necessary. Comte's own philosophy of society took general form as a theory

7

of history, and in a suggestive way he connected the development of social institutions with the improvement of the methods of human knowledge. The three stages of the development of knowledge were the theological, metaphysical, and the positive, and with each of these went a corresponding form of social organization, the military, the legalistic, and the industrial. Comte thought of himself and his associates as ushering in the third stage of knowledge, and sketched an organization of science as a "spiritual" power for that stage as well as an outline of industry for the "temporal" power. The scientists were to be the custodians of the spiritual power in the new stage and "sociology" (a term Comte invented), as the discipline dealing with all social affairs, was to be regarded as a synthetic philosophy of all the realm of knowledge. The old metaphysical philosophies were to disappear with the obsolete second stage. Bankers were to be the chiefs of the temporal power, or the industrial order, and under them, down to the proletariat, men were to select their successors, subject to the consent of their superiors. Although Comte had separated from Saint-Simon when the latter had emphasized religion, he himself went on to outline a religion of humanity with feast days, rituals, and doctrines conducive to the subordinating of man's natural egoism and the development of altruism so that the duties of citizens might be more certain of being fulfilled. The synthetic element in experience was in the emotions, and religion was to facilitate it. Rousseau had spoken, toward the end of the *Social Contract*, of a "religion of the citizen" which would strengthen the state; but the use to which religion was put by both the traditionalists and the positivists would have startled him. In reference to Comte's system J. S. Mill remarked that the pressure of society, in his plan of society, would be exerted upon the individual with a force that was truly frightful to contemplate.

Parallel with the Catholic traditionalists and the positive philosophy, various other types of emphasis upon the collectivistic basis and use of political structures developed. In England such men as Robert Owen (1771-1858) developed more proletarian theories of the collective life, as did also the Christian Socialists, Frederick Maurice (1805-1872) and Charles Kingsley (1819-1875). French collectivism of a more proletarian sort came out of Rousseau via François Babeuf (1760-1797), Comte de Saint-Simon, F. C. M. Fourier (1772-1837), P. J. Proudhon (1809-1865) and Louis Blanc (1811-1882). In Germany, deriving from Rousseau and the idealists, were "Karl Marlo" (Professor Winkelbleck, 1800-1859), R. K. Rodbertus (1805-1875) and Ferdinand Lassalle (1825-1864). Out of the left wing of the Hegelian school, under the influence of Feuerbach's materialistic interpretation, Karl Marx (1818-1883) developed his position, so dramatically stated by him in collaboration with Friedrich Engels in the *Communist Manifesto* (1848). The doctrine as stated in this and *Capital* (1867-1894) became the holy writ of the Russian Revolution of the fall of 1917, even as Rousseau had furnished by his works the proof-texts for the

French Revolution. The position of Marx involved several points: (1) the economic interpretation of history (suggestions of which were in Rousseau); (2) the theory of surplus value, according to which all the surplus value of labor above subsistence wages ultimately was to be expropriated by the owning class; (3) the doctrine that a class struggle would result from the steady increase in misery which this entailed, and that the fall of capitalism at the hands of a unified world proletariat would ensue. Marx advocated proletarian revolution through the International Workingmen's Association, and during the sixties and seventies considerable progress was made under his direction. With the dissolution of the International, however, the socialists who were Marxian in their tradition turned to action through their national political parties. The internationalism of this proletarian movement could not cope with the sentiment of nationalism as that developed in the latter part of the century. It went into decline, to be revived again in the Russian Revolution with its slogan of "Workers of the World, Unite!" And the Marxians who have ruled Russia since 1917 have gradually turned to the cultivation of their own national resources and the solving of their own Russian problems. Nationalism has been, and is (1938), triumphant over international socialism as well as over all other forms of internationalism (such as the League of Nations) in the recent past.

There was present in the nineteenth century another tradition, deriving from the previous century, which was very influential and had a most instructive career. This was the individualism of Jeremy Bentham (1748-1832), who had made a powerful engine of social criticism out of the old Lockian metaphysics, the conscious-state psychology and hedonistic ethics. His *Fragment on Government* (1776) and *Theory of Morals and Legislation* (1789) enunciated the principle of "the greatest happiness to the greatest number" (a principle to be found in Plato) as the touchstone of social reform. Bentham thought that individualistic *laissez faire* in economics served this greatest happiness of mankind, and he held to this as a subordinate principle. He justified democracy in his thinking by reasoning that by its procedures the interests of the governed and the governors were made to coincide. Hedonistic psychology and the utilitarian principle combined to argue that all people wanted happiness and, if they ruled themselves, they would approve policies which would bring that happiness.

James Mill (1773-1836), Bentham's most influential immediate follower and interpreter, adopted this same reasoning with reference to democracy, and argued to justify and strengthen the Benthamic position throughout his various writings. More influential, however, was the philosophy of his son, who was one of the clearest minds of the nineteenth century.

John Stuart Mill (1806-1873) received at the hands of his father a very thorough training in the best current traditions of English culture. As a result of early and careful coaching he felt, as he expressed it in his

*Autobiography* (1873), that in fact he began his intellectual life "a quarter of a century ahead" of his contemporaries. At all events, throughout a long and varied intellectual career Mill reacted to practically all the social traditions current in nineteenth-century thought with a sensitivity which indicated the very nicest intellectual aplomb. He began as a Benthamite, but under the influence of the German ideas which animated such men as Carlyle and Coleridge he moved toward the historical and romantic viewpoint so far that he could speak of the state as a mutual insurance society and even argue that a state was impossible without national character. He was interested in the Saint-Simonians, corresponded with Auguste Comte, against whom he reacted violently, and gradually developed an individualism very different from that of Bentham. The last book of his *Logic* (1843) indicates how much his social position differed from Bentham. He moved away from the very notion of an absolute system of political economy and championed relative and historical formulations of social laws. Social science demanded not an absolute system, but a methodology which would make possible the production of such social systems as the historical situations demanded. In his *Liberty* (1859) he made a plea for the freedom of the individual, both in thought and in action, so far as that action does not interfere with the equal liberty of others. In *Representative Government* (1861) he discussed the methods of democratic government and championed wide popular franchise and the rights of minorities. Mill so altered the metaphysical and psychological individualism of his father and Bentham as to reach a moral individualism. He came to treat individuality not as a premise but as an end to be achieved. Exceptional individuals lead the way; they cannot force the majority, but they must be conserved and allowed to differ. The influence of Mill was very great; it was shared by him at Oxford with T. H. Green, where it used to be said that one was either "takin' Green or went through the Mill."

One other outstanding thinker added to the individualistic tradition in the nineteenth century, Herbert Spencer (1820-1903). This prolific writer carried through from the eighteenth-century writings the belief in natural harmony. Nature was a perfect balance of forces; the best that man could do was to conform. *Laissez faire* had been a simple deduction from this optimistic view of the world; and it is *laissez faire* with which Spencer emerges in the nineteenth century, and which he aggressively promulgates. As biology came in he changed the "individual" into the "organism," "nature" into "the environment," and "progress" into "evolution." But the story continued to be the same. Nature was doing all it could; deliberate attempts to help social matters by way of social planning could be nothing but meddling, and the state should be restricted to the rôle of keeping each one from interfering with others in getting the natural consequences of their own action. Spencer believed implicitly in the Lamarckian doctrine of the inheritance of acquired characteristics and in evolution as a natural necessity. There was a natural law of social justice (that each should get the consequences of his own actions) and any positive action by the state would be an artificial tampering with the functioning of this law. Inevitably, given these premises, Spencer interpreted the functions of the state in the negative manner indicated. Everything was happening for the best according to the laws of cause and effect; planning by use of means and ends was worse than useless.

But the traditions of the nineteenth century were moving the other way. In England not only was T. H. Green (1836-1882) interpreting the collective state theory of the German tradition, chiefly by a Kantian emphasis, to be followed later by the Hegelianism of Bernard Bosanquet's *Philosophical Theory of the State* (1899), but, on the Continent, both the traditions of idealism and of proletarian collectivism flourished; the latter was well illustrated by a revamping of Marxism in the *Evolutionary Socialism* (1899) of Edward Bernstein. In England an indigenous collectivism emerged with the founding of the Fabian Society in 1884 (*Fabian Essays in Socialism*, 1889). Among its better known members were Bernard Shaw, Sidney Webb, and Graham Wallas. Fabianism owed a debt to Benthamism with its emphasis on "the greatest good to the greatest number." The Fabians were intellectuals who had "gone through the Mill" and then read *Das Kapital*, in which Marx had depicted so vividly the seamy side of nineteenth-century English industrial life.

Fabianism championed a form of state socialism, but took effect chiefly in municipal affairs. The activities of the society have continued to the present day.

Not only did the "greatest happiness" principle of Bentham's ethics work toward collectivistic interpretations of the nation-state, but historical emphasis on the development of institutional forms and biological ideas of evolution, with their attendant organismic analogies, all worked together toward collectivistic interpretations of social institutions. Such intellectual lumber, when confronted with the practical difficulties of late nineteenth-century economic life, the stresses and injustices of a rapidly changing industrial and power age, inevitably framed itself into various collectivistic theories of the nation-state. With hope in their eyes men turned to the nation-state, as they had with ever-increasing insistence since the sixteenth century; this time not primarily for internal peace or protection of property. Those objectives had been achieved. But they sought the organization of the multiplex utilities of a composite industrial life, the intricacies of which had become tremendously increased by the accretions of goods and services yielded by the development of applied science. To what organization, other than the state, could they turn to settle disputes and organize services?

Varying degrees of practical employment of the institution of the state obtained in the various groups of occidental culture at the end of the nineteenth century. With varying degrees of optimism the intellectual class felt that the old Aristotelian goal of "the good life" might be achieved, if not by voluntary adjustments, then by juristic arbitrament within the state, or by direct assumption of increasing functions by the state. Of course there was a fringe of dissenters, who either championed anarchistic individualism here and there, or who warned of international troubles to come; but they were regarded, for the most part, as a "lunatic fringe." Man had come so far and learned so much that it seemed inconceivable that he should ever find his whole happiness in jeopardy. With Victorian urbanity, disturbed by a minimum of hesitation, the century closed.

## CHAPTER VIII

## CONTEMPORARY VIEWPOINTS

The events of the first three decades of the twentieth century are still fresh in the memory of living men. How far the optimistic hopes of the Victorian age erred has become a matter of tragic record.

The present is always opaque, and the motives of men are perennially obscure even to themselves. The difficulties attending historical interpretation in the field of ideas increases almost by geometrical progression as the present day is approached, until one comes to the maelstrom of conflicting contemporary interests and ideas. The incoherency becomes progressively more radical. This has always been the case; as the historian approaches the present he tends to lose his historical bearings. A point in the past has a "before" and an "after" which give it a pivotal significance and historical luminosity as part of a continuity. The present has only a "before"; the "after" has not arrived. In times of rapid change the future is not only cloudy but becomes utterly black. Lord Grey expressed this as war broke in the fall of 1914, "The lights are going out all over Europe."

As an important part of the business of interpretation it is worth while to recall that the wants of men and their philosophies should be kept separate as the analysis proceeds. It must not be assumed that men who want the same thing will use the same arguments for it, or that men who use identical terminology necessarily are seeking the same ends. Philosophies are traditions which are current and available for whatever uses the particular thinker may derive from them. There is always, therefore, an element of historical motivation in the use of any set of ideas, although radical changes of doctrine may take place and great borrowing of ideas be conspicuous.

At the turn of the century several broad traditions were available and operative. (1) There was the German idealistic tradition of nationalism, dominant in its various forms in Central Europe and influential even in England and the United States. In its most significant political form it can be regarded as an interpretation of the Hegelian philosophy of history. Nation-states and their struggles were seen as the dynamic of history; every social activity was significant as it bore on nationality. This doctrine was recast in many diverse forms. (2) A second tradition was the proletarian doctrine of Marx, which placed emphasis upon the economic factors in modern life almost to the exclusion of other items. This viewpoint interpreted nationality, religion, and all other patterns of social life, in terms of economic motivation and development. A simple systematic position resulted, as precise as the formulas of the nationalists, and also couched in terms of a theory of history deriving from Hegel. In this tradition, however, the dynamic of history was seen to be a conflict of social classes. The class struggle was the pivot of movement rather than national struggle, class war rather than international war. The state tended either to be ignored or opposed (as in anarchist doctrine). (3) The third tradition was composed of the liberal-democratic doctrines of England, France, and the United States; although rooted historically in seventeenth- and eighteenth-century individualistic revolutionary philosophies, it had been subjected to certain nineteenth-century collectivistic modifications. (4) A fourth general tradition, even more submerged than the proletarian philosophies, and active frequently only as a propaganda enterprise supported by individuals, was an emerging body of international ideas. In the background lay the writings of Grotius, of the Abbé St. Pierre, Kant's *Project for Perpetual Peace,* as well as a series of tangible advances in such organizations as the Pan-American Conferences, beginning in 1889, and the Hague Conferences. The viewpoint was, in general, more consonant with the liberal-democratic tradition than with either nationalistic or communistic ideas, and its chief supporters were in England, France, and America.

The most outstanding feature of the pre-war development of political theory in this century was the attack on the theory of the absoluteness of the power of the state. This occurred in various countries and took for the most part the form of a renewed emphasis on the importance of *intermediate* forms of association. The old medieval groupings had disappeared in French and English thinking in the days of the political revolutions. The attack was delivered in theory against all

doctrines of state supremacy, whether the latter were
stated in idealistic or democratic-liberal terms; and all
the demands of subordinate groups fell on the state,
as all had fallen, hundreds of years before, on the Papacy.
Various ideas were used to justify the claim for greater
power in society which these groups, feeling themselves
at a disadvantage, wished to express. Maxime Leroy (*Les
transformations de la puissance publique*, 1907) argued
that the French *fonctionnaires* in the civil service should
become more autonomous and assume more responsibility at the expense of the power of the state. Other
syndicalists, such as Pelloutier, using the tradition of
Proudhon, or of Bergson (as with Sorel), did the same.
J. Paul-Boncour (*Le federalism economique*, 1900)
argued for a compromise between such syndicalist suggestions and the traditional French socialist position,
using the notion of "solidarity" as a basis, but championed a recognition of the increasing autonomy for
professional groups. In England A. J. Penty (*The
Restoration of the Gild System*, 1906), S. G. Hobson
(*National Guilds and the State*, 1920) and A. R. Orage
(in the *New Age*, 1911-1913) pleaded for a revival of a
guild autonomy such as the medieval ages had witnessed.
Their position resembled that of Paul-Boncour in that
it was a compromise between doctrines of state power
and syndicalism, but it added the appeal to the historical precedent of medieval society. G. D. H. Cole
was the most prolific writer in this tradition of English Guild Socialists (*Self-Government in Industry*,
1919), which championed greater participation in

power by economic groups and emphasized the contrast between producers and consumers. The guilds were the producers, and the state was thought of as "consumptive."

An interesting variation of this attack upon the absoluteness of the state appeared in the uses to which a legal doctrine was put. Otto von Gierke's *Genossenschaftstheorie* was imported into England by F. W. Maitland (see the Introduction to his translation of Gierke's *Political Theories of the Middle Ages*). It was essentially an assertion of the real personality of intermediate groups and had been dug up by Gierke and his predecessors in historical jurisprudence as a German alternative to the Roman theory of the corporation. Transplanted to England it took on new life. J. N. Figgis exploited it on behalf of the church against the state (*Churches in the Modern State*, 1913) to justify the claim for greater ecclesiastical autonomy, and H. J. Laski appealed to it in his *Authority in the Modern State* (1919) as one justification for decreasing the absoluteness of the state.

Other attacks upon the absoluteness of the state came from legal sources, and could be interpreted either as a continuation of the time-honored conflict between legislators and jurists (dating back at least to Sir Edward Coke) or as a demand for greater autonomy on the part of an intermediate group, the legal profession. The demand that *les gouvernants* be more subjected to the power of the courts is at least an insistence upon enhancing the power in society of judges as a professional group. So Leon Duguit (*Les trans-formations du droit public*, 1913, translated, by Frida and Harold Laski as *Law in the Modern State*), using the conservative French notion of "solidarity," argued for the subordination of the politicians in the state to an increased amount of legal control by the courts. Judges can elaborate their own law (see Duguit in *Modern French Legal Philosophy*, pp. 296 f.) for controlling society, independent of legislative enactments and other legal sources. Another insistence upon the prerogative of jurists came from Hugo Krabbe (*Modern Idea of the State*, 1922, translated by G. H. Sabine and W. J. Shephard), who developed the notion of the sovereignty of law within the state, implying thereby a restraining of present political powers. Krabbe went on to extend the notion to international affairs by advocating the development of international law to a position of dominance in the international situation. An adequate sovereign international law will have to be achieved as a result of the prior development of a political order which can enforce peace (a sovereign in the old sense) ; out of this domination, presumably by some all-powerful league, might come a consciousness of right on the part of all peoples which would accord to international legal rules the sovereignty which they should possess.

These and other attempts to limit the power of the state by enhancing the powers of the intermediate forms of association or by emphasis upon law, as well as the Marxian communist movement, dating from the

Second International of 1889, were placed at an increasing practical disadvantage following 1914 because of the outbreak of the World War. Wartime organization of national forces submerged intermediate associations, professional groups, and syndicates, in great national military machines; members of the International enlisted as soldiers to kill each other. The war produced a great increase in the internal power of the state as group agitation subsided.

While the exigencies of war operated to inhibit criticism of the absoluteness of the state as well as to impede practical internal movements aimed at limiting its power, they at the same time became the occasion of a flood of attacks against the philosophies of opposing states. Notably the intellectual guns of outstanding thinkers in England and America were turned upon the German idealistic theory of the state. George Santayana published his *Egotism in German Philosophy* in 1916, in which he argued that German philosophy as a whole was romantic egotism made into a metaphysics. John Dewey (*German Philosophy and Politics,* 1915) attacked the Kantian doctrine of the two contrasting worlds of nature and reason, and emphasized that the notion of the *a priori* as developed by Kant and his successors had played into the hands of the Prussian ruling class by providing an antecedent justification for whatever duties those in control of the German state could impose upon their political subordinates. The doctrine of an antecedent inner sanction operated to obscure to the German people the external con-

8

sequences of a policy of reckless opportunism in foreign affairs. Hegel's philosophy of history only intensified the sense of national destiny, irrespective of consequences; and a technically competent and scientific people were rendered visionary and egotistical fanatics in the realm of their political relations. L. T. Hobhouse (*Metaphysical Theory of the State*, 1918) made similar strictures in reference to the German tradition, centering his attack on the Hegelian philosophy. The systematic perversion of the basic distinction between facts and what ought to be, which is present in the Hegelian doctrine, distorts all thinking about social matters. Hobhouse criticized the Hegelian notion of the "concrete universal" and indicated that it completely obscured any statement of social relations since the assumption of it placed the state by definition in a position of antecedent authority. Freedom is thus seen as law, equality as discipline; and a vague statement of the problem of social relations has been perverted into its own solution.

The progressive discrediting of the idealistic political and social philosophy was furthered by all these attacks. English idealistic theory countered to the best of its ability with the rejoinders of J. H. Muirhead in *Mind* for 1924 and of B. Bosanquet in the preface of the 1920 edition of his *Philosophical Theory of the State*, in which he claimed the federalism of Mary Follett's *The New State* as an elucidation of the real idealistic position. In general, idealism retreated to the position of an ascending scale of group wills. It is obvious at once that the cultural riches ("group mind") of a national life are present neither in a minor grouping, such as a trade union, nor in an international league; the net effect has been the waning of German idealism in England and America. In Central Europe, of course, no such retreat was made by idealistic philosophy, and its metaphysical tradition based upon its antique psychology and pre-scientific anthropology continued to flourish.

In 1917 the Russian Revolution placed a proletarian tradition in control of one of the historic European state structures for the first time. Russia became communistic by the paradoxical accession to power, in the least industrial of all European countries, of men imbued with Marxian doctrines concerning the effects of the industrial revolution. It is a strange comment on Marxian doctrine that it came to power among a peasant agrarian population in the most backward area of Europe. Lenin (*The Proletarian Revolution*, 1920, and also *The State and Revolution*—see *Collected Works*) was the leader of the group which seized power in October, 1917, and announced the dictatorship of the proletariat, the one-class society, throughout all Russia. Here the class struggle was won, as it was destined to be won later elsewhere; a new International was organized (1919) and the slogan "Workers of the World, Unite" appeared even on the paper money of the new government. Dialectical materialism was asserted as the absolute doctrine, an absolute proletariat state was organized, land was given to the peasants, and

the Communist Party has ruled the country subsequently. There have been internal dissensions, efforts have
been made to facilitate industrialization and education;
the third constitution of the U.S.S.R. went into effect
January 1, 1937. The Russian system has been praised
by proletarians the world over, and condemned with
equal vigor by all reactionary groups. Its intolerant
revolutionary fanaticism has offended democratic
liberals; its aggressive propaganda has produced
tremendous flutterings in all the Tory hencoops of
Western Europe, to which it has appeared as "the big
bad wolf." The fact seems to have been that Russia
prior to 1917, because of its development, had no
middle class (85 per cent of the population were
peasants); when the stress of the World War broke
down the old aristocratic, almost feudal, officialdom,
the control of the society fell through to the first level
at which there were groups well enough organized to
control public affairs. This happened to be a small
group of Russians, chiefly industrial workers and earlier
revolutionaries, who were indoctrinated with Marxian
philosophy. Hence the paradox of an arbitrary industrial philosophy, developed as a dialectical materialism out of the left wing of Hegelianism, written into
the constitution of a peasant agricultural country.

While Eastern Europe went fanatically communist,
the victorious Allies in the World War organized the
League of Nations at the Paris Conference. Internationalism emerged on the wave of pacific feeling
generated by years of horrible sacrifice and suffering.

Woodrow Wilson was the leading personality in writing the Covenant of the League of Nations into the Treaty of Versailles; his public utterances and the document itself are the best expressions of the philosophy involved. The literature has become tremendous. The official League publications themselves constitute a small library. The hope of permanent peace in the hearts of men combined with the hope of permanent hegemony in the minds of the victors. Nationalism during the war had been triumphant; all nations had become progressively regimented for military purposes. It was a tired, a nervous, a desperate, but a victorious nationalism which emerged. State officials were at the peak of their power in modern society. The international experiment of a world government was launched at the very time when some governments which, in the nature of the situation, it had to control were at their maximum development. In the brief retrospect available it seems as if the League had a minimum chance of survival from the start. "In time of peace prepare for war" is a slogan which internationalists should revise to read, "In time of peace prepare the machinery to prevent war." Article X was almost as much an anachronism as Henry VIII would have been in the days of Innocent III, or the great Innocent in the age of Diocletian. The League remains as the symbol of a great hope. It has functioned too much as a league of victors, but its possibilities are apparent and its future is still in the making. Although some of the League's machinery has never been utilized, and other parts of it are falling into disuse in the present situation, the fact remains that the philosophy of internationalism has received in this century an embodiment in actually existing political machinery incomparably greater than that witnessed by any previous period in modern history. International government has a foothold in reality, albeit a precarious one.

Of course, had the post-war trend toward democracy in Central Europe not been reversed by the rise of dictatorships, or had the United States joined the League of Nations at its beginning, the subsequent history of Europe, and of the world, would have been radically different.

The most outstanding development of the last few years has been the intensification of nationalistic tradition in Central Europe accompanied by the progressive ascendancy to military power of Italy and Germany. Fascism has been followed by Nazism. In Italy there was great disappointment following the Treaty of Versailles because greater rewards had not been given to the Italian people. Economic disorders in the early twenties enabled a group of aggressive men under the leadership of Mussolini to seize control of the machinery of government and abolish such parliamentary procedures as the Italians had employed. A personal dictatorship has resulted which operates in terms of a peculiar fusion of German idealistic tradition (Alfred Rocco, *The Political Doctrine of Fascism*), Machiavellian methods, and dreams derived from the ancient glories of the Roman Empire. The state is asserted to be a spiritual and ethical entity; no human or spiritual values can exist outside it (Mussolini, *The Doctrine of Fascism*, 1935). Fascism denies all democratic ideologies, both in premise and application. It rejects all pacifism and internationalism and emphasizes the nobility of war. The Fascist philosophy, developed after the march on Rome, out-Hegels Hegel in its idealistic nationalism, translates Machiavelli's advice to a Medician prince into national policies (this was almost a work of supererogation!) quotes for further justification the pantheistic, nationalistic rhapsodies of Mazzini, and champions a totalitarian state controlled by an *élite* which, by common understanding, is composed of those who enunciate the doctrine.

Nazi Germany has had a similar career. The constitutional federated republic which was set up under the Weimar Constitution has been displaced by a dictatorship under Adolph Hitler. Republican Germany made the mistake of tolerating a private army within the state. Violence and terrorism were introduced into internal politics and, after a certain point had been passed, the maintenance of democratic constitutional procedures became impossible. Hitler and his private army seized the state, and have maintained their control subsequently. The "purge" of June 30, 1934, illustrates the method of the Nazis in handling the opposition. Hitler admitted that 77 were killed; the *Manchester Guardian* claimed that 282 were executed. Subsequent estimates have raised the amount to figures as high as 1,200. The usual justifications for ruthlessness appear

(Hitler, *My Battle;* Konrad Heiden, *History of National Socialism*), and the romantic egotism of German philosophy reappears again in a hodgepodge of idealistic phraseology about the German nature and its march through history (Hermann Schwartz, *Zur philosophischen Grundlegung des Nationalsozialismus*). The Leader and the Party are to be the instruments of the further self-expansion of the German Spirit. There is a Fichte Society in Germany for the spreading of the authentic Nazi doctrine; the continuity of idealistic tradition is apparent. The Aryan myth, anti-Semitism, anti-Communism, and a grandiose pageantry are mixed in inextricable confusion with the idealistic metaphysical philosophy of history in the Nazi mentality. The German soul must have its own culture, economy, religion; and the Totalitarian state is the be-all and end-all for which the youth are to be educated. Outside the state there is no salvation. A new national drama of salvation emerges as a reborn Pan-Germanism with its *Drang nach Osten.*

It would be unfair to all dictatorships not to recognize that strong government has always been the prescription for disorder. The chief argument for the League of Nations Covenant was that a "strong" government was needed to prevent international anarchy. Italian and German, as well as Russian, revolutionary dictatorships may be regarded from this angle as counsels of desperation in a world disordered by the great catastrophe of the World War. Wartime regimentation, prolonged for years in the war period,

economic need, wounded egotism, private ambition, en-
during hate, and paranoiac fear, all have played their
part in the remarkable recent decadence of Europe.
More complete understanding of how it came about
brings fuller realization of the agony, the pathos, the
raw and unappeased human needs, the desperation and
the futility, which is contemporary Europe. Economic
need in an economy of scarcity may have contributed
to the regimentation; if that be so, it is regimentation
such as food administrators used in the World War,
food rationing and all that goes with it, not a paradise
of plenty. Societies which have become glorified camps
can scarcely pose as economic ideals for either the
workers or the industrial managers of those democratic
communities which have within their grasp the achievement, by proper organization, of an economy of plenty.
Personal dictatorship is—personal dictatorship. It is
neither the triumph of scientific business management
and engineering science nor a utopian dream come true.
Personal dictatorship means what it has always meant
since man became man—tyranny, supported by as-
sassinations, "purges," and desperate internal violence
as conflicts develop over the question of who shall be
the one to exercise the supreme authority. It brings to
the top the cunning psychopath, the megalomaniac with
the gleam of a secret enthusiasm in his eye, the exhibi-
tionist with an oracular voice and a flair for pageantry.
The understanding of all this, however, does not make
it easier to endure; madness is madness, however it came
about. To deny that it is, is more madness. The dictators

may not be mad, of course; it may be merely that Aristotle's famous remark about the people of Miletus is applicable to them, "They are not fools, but they do the things that fools do." However that may be, nineteenth-century nationalism, which had been a vocation, a culture, a destiny, and a religion, became in the twentieth century a psychosis—an inferiority complex, a delusion of grandeur, and a collective paranoia.

What of the liberal-democratic tradition which is still operative in England, France and the United States? If Communists, on the one hand, and Fascists and Nazis, on the other, are to be believed, democracy is an outmoded doctrine and a middle-class illusion of the decadent past. Liberalism with its insistence upon free discussion and debate is a futile gesture and has definitely lost the initiative.

Has the liberal-democratic tradition lost the initiative? Military events, the rearming of Germany, the breaking of treaty agreements, Ethiopia, Austria— these events indicate that at least one type of initiative is in the possession of the dictatorships. Democracies are slower in action and wait for an approaching unanimity of attitude before plunging into adventures in violence. It should be recalled that the World War began in Central Europe. But military initiative must not be confused with cultural initiative. The desperado who draws a gun always has the military initiative. Caution in the use of violence is not an evidence of weakness so much as it is of good sense. Autocrats would do well to remember that hesitation on the part of democratic countries may be the result of neither lack of confidence in their institutions nor fear of the ultimate result of an arbitrament of arms. There is an old saying to the effect that only "fools rush in."

But where is the "cultural initiative"? What has provided the dynamic in modern occidental society? Is it in a dialectic of national states, as Hegel and his current shabby imitators have held? Or is it in a class war as envisaged by the exponents of the dialectical materialism of Marx? For the liberal-democrat both of these positions present a complete misstatement of the significant developments of modern culture (J. Dewey, *Liberalism and Social Action*, 1935). The dynamic is not in those conflicts which have brought recent civilization to the brink of disaster. It lies rather in the enormous development of modern scientific control over natural forces. Technical science is the distinguishing feature of contemporary culture. The cultural initiative lies at the point of the cultivation and extension-in-use of scientific methodology. This is the exclusive possession of no nation and of no class. Democratic procedures, with their assumption of toleration, mutual confidence, freedom of discussion, deliberation, and ultimate devices for decisions on personnel and policies are simply the most nearly scientific that have yet been organized by man in the sphere of government. The cultural initiative lies with the liberal-democratic tradition in that it approaches most closely to scientific procedures in social affairs. The ballot signalized the introduction of statistical methods as substitutes for violence.

Democracies count heads instead of breaking them. While democratic theorists have few illusions about the perfection of the societies in which they live, they argue that all other political forms have been tried and found worse. To abandon democracy would be to renounce all the political sagacity acquired by the English since the Long Parliament and by the French since 1789. When democratic procedures have broken down, as in the American Civil War, irretrievable loss has occurred. Democratic methods have proved their worth in terms of that long-run efficiency which is the sole test of a form of government. The liberal-democratic tradition cherishes the results of the scientific and industrial advances of modern society. Its confidence is not a faith in an absolute formula, but reliance upon scientific method. It does not prate of historical destiny, but seeks the goal of a good life for all. It does not believe in an automatic evolution by blind class or national conflict, but prizes the competency and validity of its procedures.

The alternatives by way of social organization are not confined, consequently, to left-wing Communistic dictatorship, and right-wing Totalitarian dictatorship. Both these have produced societies based on prescientific myths and shibboleths, in which political control is maintained by "purges." They have turned their backs on modern science, abridged the freedom of investigation and speech, and sabotaged their institutions of higher learning. They have reverted to book-burning and witch-hunting. Any good features which they possess are accidental rather than essential. The third alternative is a society utilizing investigation, experimentation, and the calm consideration of policies to be adopted, a society regarding the business of living together as an applied science, which, by responsible civilized processes, will put the mechanical means of abundance at the disposal of all.

Both doctrinaire Marxian socialism in Russia, and German idealism, which has become more nationalistically mystical and fatuous in Fascism and Nazism, have opposed to them the liberal-democratic tradition of the Western democracies. These are attempting to become progressively more scientific. The devotion of the democracies to modern science and education is at once an evidence of their insight, the basis of their morale, and an augury of their future. The initiative in modern culture has passed to them by default.

# SELECTED BIBLIOGRAPHY

I. SECONDARY SOURCES

(Bibliographies of these works will indicate detailed primary sources.)

Barker, Ernest. *Greek Political Theory: Plato and His Predecessors.* London, Methuen and Company, rev. ed., 1918.
———. *Political Thought in England from Herbert Spencer to the Present Day.* New York, Henry Holt and Company, 1915.
———. *Political Thought of Plato and Aristotle, The.* New York, G. Putnam's Sons, 1906.
Barnes, Harry E. *Sociology and Political Theory, a Consideration of the Sociological Basis of Politics.* New York, A. A. Knopf, 1924.
Bonar, James. *Philosophy and Political Economy in Some of Their Historical Relations.* London, G. Allen & Unwin, 3rd ed., 1922. Also in the "Library of Philosophy," 1927.
Brown, Ivor. *English Political Theory.* London, Methuen and Company, 1925.
Burns, C. Delisle. *Political Ideals, Their Nature and Development.* London and New York, Oxford University Press, 3rd ed., 1919.
Carlyle, Robert W., and Carlyle, A. J. *A History of Medieval Political Theory in the West.* 6 vols. Edinburgh and London, W. Blackwood & Sons, 1928-1936.
Coker, Francis W. *Recent Political Thought.* New York and London, D. Appleton-Century Company, 1934.
Cook, Thomas I. *History of Political Philosophy from Plato to Burke.* New York, Prentice-Hall, 1936.
Davidson, William L. *Political Thought in England, the Utilitarians from Bentham to J. S. Mill.* New York, Henry Holt and Company, 1915, 1916. Also, London, T. Butterworth, Ltd., 5th impression, 1935.
Dicey, A. V. *Lectures on the Relation between Law and Public Opinion in England during the Nineteenth Century.* New York, The Macmillan Company, 2nd ed., 1914.
Doyle, Phyllis. *A History of Political Thought.* London, J. Cape, 1933.
Dunning, W. A. *A History of Political Theories, Ancient and Medieval.* New York, The Macmillan Company, 1902, 1930.

——. *A History of Political Theories, from Luther to Montesquieu.* New York, The Macmillan Company, 1905, 1928, 1931.

——. *A History of Political Theories, from Rousseau to Spencer.* New York, The Macmillan Company, 1920, 1926, 1928.

Ellwood, Charles A. *A History of Social Philosophy.* New York, Prentice-Hall, 1938.

Engelmann, Géza. *Political Philosophy from Plato to Jeremy Bentham.* Translated from the German by K. F. Geiser. New York and London, Harper and Brothers, 1927.

Flint, Robert. *History of the Philosophy of History.* Edinburgh, W. Blackwood & Sons, 1893.

Gettel, Raymond G. *History of Political Thought.* New York and London, The Century Company, 1924.

Gide, Charles, and Rist, Charles. *A History of Economic Doctrines from the Time of the Physiocrats to the Present Day.* Translated from the 2nd rev. and augm. ed. of 1913 . . . by R. Richards. London, G. G. Harrap & Company, 1915. Also Boston, D. C. Heath and Company [19..].

Gooch, G. P. *Political Thought in England from Bacon to Halifax.* London, Williams and Norgate, 1914–1915. Also, New York, Henry Holt and Company, 1914.

Hearnshaw, F. J. C. *The Development of Political Ideas.* Garden City, N. Y., Doubleday, Doran, and Company, 1928.

——. (Also the editor of a useful series of studies of various periods by miscellaneous writers.)

Janet, Paul. *Histoire de la science politique dans ses rapports avec la morale.* Paris, Libraire Felix Alcan, 5th ed., 1925.

Joad, C. E. M. *Modern Political Theory.* Oxford, The Clarendon Press, 1924.

Laski, Harold J. *Political Thought in England from Locke to Bentham.* New York, Henry Holt and Company, 1920.

Leighton, Joseph A. *Social Philosophies in Conflict; Fascism and Nazism, Communism, Liberal Democracy.* New York and London, D. Appleton-Century Company, 1937.

MacCunn, John. *Six Radical Thinkers: Bentham, J. S. Mill, Cobden, Carlyle, Mazzini, T. H. Green.* London, E. Arnold, 1907, 1910.

McIlwain, Charles H. *The Growth of Political Thought in the West, from the Greeks to the End of the Middle Ages.* New York, The Macmillan Company, 1932.

Merriam, C. E., and Barnes, H. E., eds. *A History of Political*

*Theories, Recent Times.* New York, The Macmillan Company, 1924.

Murray, Robert H. *A History of Political Science from Plato to the Present.* New York, D. Appleton and Company, 1926.

Pollock, Frederick. *An Introduction to the History of the Science of Politics.* London, Macmillan and Company, Ltd., new rev. ed., 1911.

Poole, Reginald L. *Illustrations of the History of Medieval Thought and Learning.* New York, The Macmillan Company, 2nd ed. rev., 1920.

Richard, Gaston. *La question sociale et le mouvement philosophique au XIX⁰ siècle.* Paris, A. Colin, 1914.

Rockow, Lewis. *Contemporary Political Thought in England.* London, L. Parsons, 1925.

Russell, Bertrand. *Freedom versus Organization, 1814-1914.* New York, W. W. Norton, 1934.

Sabine, George H. *A History of Political Theory.* New York, Henry Holt and Company, 1937.

Vaughn, Charles E. *Studies in the History of Political Philosophy.* London and New York, Longmans, Green and Company, 1925.

Willoughby, W. W. *The Political Theories of the Ancient World.* New York, Longmans, Green and Company, 1903.

Zimmern, A. E. *The Greek Commonwealth; Politics and Economics in Fifth-Century Athens.* Oxford, The Clarendon Press, 5th ed. rev., 1931.

II. A SUGGESTED READING LIST OF PRIMARY SOURCES FOR THE BEGINNING STUDENT

The following titles are arranged in the order in which they are discussed in the text. For the contemporary works, publication facts are given. The others may be found in Everyman's Library, the Loeb Classical Library, the Home University Library of Modern Knowledge, and other similar lists.

Plato. (1) *Republic;* (2) *Statesman;* (3) *Laws.*
Aristotle. (1) *Nicomachean Ethics;* (2) *Politics.*
Polybius. *History of Rome,* Bk. VI.
Cicero. (1) *On the Laws;* (2) *On the Republic.*
Augustine. *The City of God.*
Marsiglio of Padua. *Defensor Pacis.*
Machiavelli. *The Prince.*

## 122  BIBLIOGRAPHY

Bodin, Jean. *Six Books Concerning the State.*
Hobbes, Thomas. *Leviathan.*
Spinoza, Benedict. *Tractatus Politicus.*
Locke, John. *Civil Government* (second treatise).
Rousseau, J. J. *The Social Contract.*
Bentham, Jeremy. (1) *Fragment on Government;* (2) *Theory of Morals and Legislation.*
Kant, Immanuel. *Politics.*
Fichte, J. G. (1) *Characteristics of the Present Age;* (2) *Addresses to the German Nation;* (3) *Vocation of Man.*
Hegel, G. W. F. (1) *Philosophy of Right;* (2) *Philosophy of History.*
Comte, Auguste. *Positive Philosophy.*
Mill, J. S. (1) *Liberty;* (2) *Representative Government;* (3) *Autobiography.*
Spencer, Herbert. (1) *Overlegislation;* (2) *Man versus the State.*
Marx, Karl. (1) *Communist Manifesto;* (2) *Capital.*
Green, T. H. *Principles of Political Obligation.*
Bosanquet, Bernard. *Philosophical Theory of the State.*

### Twentieth-Century Writers

Cecil, Hugh. *Conservatism.* London, Williams and Norgate, 1912, Also, New York, Henry Holt and Company, 1912.
Dewey, John. *Democracy and Education; an Introduction to the Philosophy of Education.* New York, The Macmillan Company, 1916, 1929.
———. *German Philosophy and Politics.* New York, Henry Holt and Company, 1915.
———. *Liberalism and Social Action.* New York, G. P. Putnam's Sons, 1935.
———. *The Public and Its Problems.* New York, Henry Holt and Company, 1927.
Hobhouse, Leonard T. *Liberalism.* London, Williams and Norgate, 1911. Also, New York, Henry Holt and Company, 1911.
———. *The Metaphysical Theory of the State.* New York, The Macmillan Company, 1918.
Laski, Harold J. *Democracy in Crisis.* Chapel Hill, The University of North Carolina Press, 1933.
———. *Grammar of Politics, A.* New Haven, Yale University Press, 5th impression, 2nd ed., 1931.

# BIBLIOGRAPHY 123

## COLLECTIONS OF PRIMARY SOURCES

Coker, Francis W. *Readings in Political Philosophy*. New York, The Macmillan Company, rev. ed., 1938. (Ends with Bentham.)

Henderson, E. F., ed. and trans. *Select Historical Documents of the Middle Ages*. London, G. Bell and Sons, 1903.

Spahr, Margaret. *Readings in Recent Political Philosophy*. New York, The Macmillan Company, 1935.

Wagner, Donald O. *Social Reformers. Adam Smith to John Dewey*. New York, The Macmillan Company, 1934.

# INDEX

Aegidius Romanus, 41.
Alexander the Great, 18, 21, 22, 23.
Alexander III, 41.
Alexander VI, 46.
Althusius, Johannes, 55.
Ambrose, Saint, 37.
Aquinas, Thomas, *See* THOMAS AQUINAS.
Aristotle, 18-21, 22, 45.
Augustine, Saint, Bishop of Hippo, 37-38.

Babeuf, François, 91.
Bentham, Jeremy, 58, 93, 94, 97.
Bergson, Henri, 102.
Bernard of Clairvaux, Saint, 41.
Bernstein, Edward, 96.
Blanc, Louis, 91.
Bodin, Jean, 54-55, 62, 83.
Bonald, Louis de, 87-88.
Boniface VIII, 44.
Bosanquet, Bernard, 96, 106.
Burke, Edmund, 87.

Calvin, John, 52.
Charles the Great, 39.
Charles I, 59, 64.
Charles VIII, 46.
Charles IX, 53.
Cicero, 29-30.
Cleisthenes, 10.
Cole, G. D. H., 102.
Comte, Auguste, 89-91, 94.
Conciliar Movement, 42, 64, 65.
Constantine I, 35, 36.
Cromwell, Oliver, 59, 61.

Decius, 35.
Dewey, John, 105, 115.
Diocletian, 35, 109.
Dubois, Peter, 45.
Duguit, Leon, 104.
Dunning, W. A., 71.
Duplessis-Mornay, Philippe, 52.

Elizabeth, Queen, 77.
Engels, Friedrich, 91.
Epictetus, 26.
Epicureanism, 25, 26.
Epicurus, 24.

Fabian Society, 96.
Ferdinand V, 47.
Fichte, J. G., 79-80.
Figgis, J. N., 103.
Follett, Mary, 106.
Fourier, F. C. M., 91.
Frederick I, 41.
Frederick II, 41.

Gentilis, Albericus, 57.
German Idealism, 83, 117.
Gierke, Otto von, 55, 103.
Green, T. H., 96.
Gregory VII, 41.
Gregory IX, 41.
Grey, Edward, Lord, 99.
Grimm, Jacob and Wilhelm, 83.
Grotius, Hugo, 56, 57, 101.
Guild Socialists, 102.

Hadrian IV, 41.
Hegel, G. W. F., 81-82, 88, 106, 108.

www.ingramcontent.com/pod-product-compliance
Lightning Source LLC
Chambersburg PA
CBHW030654270326
41929CB00007B/361